Prevention RD's Cooking and Baking with Almond Flour

Skyhorse Publishing books may be purchased in bulk at special discounts for sales promotion, corporate gifts, fund-raising, or educational purposes. Special editions can also be created to specifications. For details, contact the Special Sales Department, Skyhorse Publishing, 307 West 36th Street, 11th Floor, New York, NY 10018 or info@skyhorsepublishing.com.

Skyhorse® and Skyhorse Publishing® are registered trademarks of Skyhorse Publishing, Inc.®, a Delaware corporation.

www.skyhorsepublishing.com

10 9 8 7 6 5 4 3 2

Library of Congress Cataloging-in-Publication Data is available on file.

Paperback ISBN: 978-1-5107-4787-6
Ebook ISBN: 978-1-62914-309-5

Cover design by Danielle Ceccolini
Cover photos by Nicole Morrissey

Printed in China

Prevention RD's
Cooking and Baking with Almond Flour

Quick and Easy Meals for a Gluten-Free Diet

Nicole Morrissey

Founder of *Prevention RD*
Registered Dietitian and Diabetes Educator

Skyhorse Publishing

Contents

Acknowledgments

When I moved to Ohio, I started a job working in a dialysis unit as a renal dietitian. I was going through new-hire orientation and was no more than two hours into my first day when in walked Donna, this tall, stunning brunette in a perfectly pressed pencil skirt and suit jacket. I already knew: this woman was a mover and shaker.   By the end of that morning, Donna had not only introduced herself, but she had let me in on her entrepreneurial endeavors. I could tell this woman was smart, powerful, and ready to take on the nutrition world by storm.

Donna and I clicked immediately. Just a few years younger than my mom and with the energy and looks of a woman in her twenties, we were two peas in a pod. We were constantly brainstorming our next business project, coming up with ways we could be our own bosses and truly change people's lives.

Together, Donna and I shared in many successes and failures—some big, some small. We marketed ourselves to medical providers and practices of all sizes everywhere between Columbus and Cleveland, spending countless hours and many dollars with few opportunities coming to fruition. Why didn't these providers see the value in nutrition for their patients? Being a dietitian in private practice was hard work, but it was rewarding and a learning experience I wouldn't trade for anything. At lunch, Donna and I would meet in the small town of Marion, Ohio, at this little diner packed with small-town charm. We would order our soup and salad and talk far too long for a lunch break . . . and then argue over who was going to pay.

From the moment Donna learned about my blog, she would always ask me how it was going. She would sing my praises to her patients, her friends, and her family. Yet, to this day, I'm not sure Donna even knows what a blog actually is—she's not exactly the computer type. However, she does know what a cookbook is, and ever since I signed on for my first cookbook, she has told me every time we talk how proud she is of me.

Donna, I'm so proud of you, too. To a woman who showed me what it's like to support and surround myself with strong people, not to feel threatened by them. To a woman who has laughed with me until we've cried—literally. To a woman who lives and breathes nutrition in her own life and has inspired thousands to do the same. To a woman who is honorable, wise, and caring beyond words. To a woman I call one of my dearest friends and who makes me a better person by simply being part of my life. Donna, this book is for you.

Introduction

Dietitians can be very type-A and "inside the box." I can say this because I'm a dietitian, and because it's often true. We like to know the latest research and put our critical thinking hats on. We're typically smart (can I say that without sounding pretentious?) . . . but we have our areas of expertise, just like anyone else. When people ask us nutrition-related questions, we feel we should know the answers to . . . all of them. Truth is, nutrition is a very young science. We are learning more each and every day about food, food processing, and all the intricacies between health and food.

The relationship between gluten and its effects on people remains a fairly large question mark. I feel confident that we're only scratching the surface with what we know about Celiac disease, gluten intolerance, and gluten sensitivity. The years to come will help expand on the foundation of what we know today: some people are healthier and more physically comfortable without gluten in their diets.

There are quickly emerging reasons for gluten-free living, including Celiac disease, gluten intolerance, and gluten sensitivity. In those with adverse reactions to gluten, unpleasant gastrointestinal side effects, malabsorption, anemia, delayed growth, infertility, and various cancers are of great concern. In the United States, it is estimated that 1 in 133 people (about 1 percent) of the population are diagnosed with Celiac disease. Statistically, women and European-descent Americans are at highest risk. Incidence of Celiac disease increases with age. It is widely accepted that both

Gluten-Free	NOT Gluten-Free
Amaranth	Barley
Arrowroot	Bulgar
Bean flours (garbanzo, etc.)	Couscous
Buckwheat	Spelt
Corn	Durum
Fava beans	Farina
Hominy	Farro
Legumes	Kamut
Millet	Malt (extract, flavoring, syrup, vinegar)
Nuts and nut flours/meals	Matzoh
Oats (uncontaminated)	Oats (most commercial brands)
Quinoa	Orzo
Rice	Rye
Sorghum flour	Semolina
Soy	Wheat (bran, germ, starch)
Tapioca	
Teff	

genetics and environmental factors play a role in the development of Celiac disease. Elimination of gluten from the diet is the only effective treatment, which has led to the rapid rise of gluten-free foods, recipes, and menu offerings.

Am I a gluten-free expert? Not in the least. Pretty far from it, actually. In fact, I don't even live a gluten-free lifestyle . . . or at least, I do not as of today. What I do know is that I love good, healthy food, I'm proficient in the kitchen, and I've been curious about gluten-free living, cooking, and baking for as long as I can remember. As a registered dietitian, I have had patients who seek my advice for adhering to a gluten-free lifestyle, and, before now, I was doing an injustice to both them and myself with my lack of gluten-free knowledge when it comes to the foods we eat and make.

I've learned one thing for sure through writing this cookbook: gluten-free cooking and baking is tough! But, it can be done and done well. Unfortunately, the amount of time, ingredients, and frustration can be taxing to perfect gluten-free cooking and baking, which is why I am truly humbled by the gluten-free community and honored to offer you this book to add to your gluten-free repertoire of recipes.

Before creating this book, I had only played around a time or two with almond flour. While its wholesome nutrition speaks for itself, I had no idea how truly versatile, moist, flavorful, and delicious it could be. It has been thoroughly enjoyable to learn the idiosyncrasies of cooking and baking with almond flour and, in the end, I prevailed! I have mastered the art of almond flour, and I want to help you do the same . . . whether you're gluten-free, seeking a lower carbohydrate diet, or simply wish to increase the nutrition in your diet—almond flour has a place at your table.

Look for These Icons

You will see the icons below on various recipes included in this collection. They will indicate whether a recipe is vegetarian, vegan, dairy-free, and more. You can also use these icons to spot meals that are perfect for anyone following a Paleo or low-carb diet.

 SUGAR-FREE: no natural or artificial sweeteners used, including honey or maple syrup

 PALEO: grain-free and dairy-free, following Paleolithic guidelines

 VEGETARIAN: no meat, poultry, or seafood

 VEGAN: no animal product, including dairy, eggs, and honey

 LOW-CARB: defined as less than 15.0 grams of carbohydrate per serving

 HIGH-FIBER: defined as greater than or equal to 5.0 grams of fiber per serving

 DAIRY-FREE: no animal dairy or butter

Breakfasts

Coconut-Oat Cranberry Breakfast Cookies

3 cups almond flour

3 cups gluten-free old fashioned
    oats

2 teaspoons baking soda

1½ teaspoons salt

1 tablespoon cinnamon

¾ cup brown sugar

2 eggs

¼ cup olive oil

1¼ cup unsweetened
    applesauce

½ cup unsweetened dried
    cranberries

½ cup unsweetened coconut
    flakes

Directions:

Preheat oven to 350° F. Line three baking sheets with parchment paper and set aside.

In a large bowl, whisk together the almond flour, oats, baking soda, salt, cinnamon, and sugar; set aside.

In a medium bowl, lightly beat the eggs. To the eggs, whisk in the oil and applesauce.

Fold the wet ingredients into the dry. The almond flour will slowly absorb the liquid and will become cookie batter–like. Fold in the cranberries and coconut.

Using a ¼-cup portion, scoop batter onto cookie sheets, allowing 2 inches between cookies. Slightly flatten the cookies into ¾-inch thick, round cookies. Bake for 20–22 minutes or until golden. Allow to cool on baking sheet for several moments before transferring to a wire cooling rack to cool completely. Serve warm or at room temperature. Leftover cookies can be frozen for up to 6 months.

Yield: 22 cookies

Nutrition Information (per cookie):

209 calories; 12.6 g. fat; 17 mg. cholesterol; 280 mg. sodium; 21.6 g. carbohydrate; 3.6 g. fiber; 5.2 g. protein; 9.4 g. sugar

Cook's Comment:

Oats are a gluten-free product when they are not processed or packaged in facilities where there may be cross-contamination with wheat. Read labels closely to ensure your oats are, in fact, gluten-free.

Fluffy Buttermilk Pancakes

1¾ cup blanched almond flour
1 tablespoon granulated sugar
1 teaspoon baking powder
¼ teaspoon salt
Pinch of cinnamon

3 eggs
½ teaspoon vanilla extract
1 cup low-fat buttermilk
1 tablespoon coconut oil,
   melted and cooled

Directions:

Preheat griddle or electric griddle to 375° F.

In a large bowl, whisk to combine the almond flour, sugar, baking powder, salt, and cinnamon; set aside.

In a medium bowl, lightly beat the eggs. Add the vanilla, buttermilk, and melted and cooled coconut oil; whisk well.

Pour the wet ingredients into the dry and whisk to moisten the almond flour. Allow batter to rest for 3–5 minutes.

Spoon roughly 3 tablespoons of the batter onto the preheated griddle and spread the batter to a 3- to 4-inch diameter using the back of the spoon. Repeat with remaining batter. Flip pancakes after 3–4 minutes, or when there are bubbles forming on the tops. If the pancakes wish to stick to the griddle slightly, work your way around the pancake gently with the spatula, releasing the pancake from the griddle. The pancakes should then flip easily without breaking. Cook pancakes an additional 2–3 minutes after flipping. Repeat with remaining batter in batches. Serve hot.

Yield: 10 pancakes (5 servings; 2 pancakes each)

Nutrition Information (per serving):

321 calories; 25.8 g. fat; 113 mg. cholesterol; 299 mg. sodium; 13.2 g. carbohydrate; 4.2 g. fiber; 13.6 g. protein; 6.2 g. sugar

Cook's Comment:

Due to the lack of gluten, these pancakes can be a little tricky to flip. Be sure to keep the pancakes small in size and do not undercook before flipping.

Mushroom, Asparagus, and Gruyere Quiche

<u>Crust</u>:

2 cups blanched almond flour

¼ teaspoon salt

1 egg

2 tablespoons cold unsalted butter, cubed

<u>Filling</u>:

1 teaspoon extra-virgin olive oil

8 oz. baby bella mushrooms, sliced

10 oz. fresh asparagus, woody ends trimmed and cut into 2-inch pieces

½ teaspoon salt, divided

¼ teaspoon black pepper, divided

6 eggs

¼ cup nonfat milk

3 oz. gruyere cheese, shredded

Directions:

Preheat oven to 350° F. Spray a ceramic pie pan with cooking spray and set aside.

To prepare the crust, pulse the almond flour and salt together in a food processor several times. Add the egg and cold butter and continue to process until the mixture looks moist and pebbly; transfer the crust to the pan. Using your hands, press the dough into the pan and work the dough up the sides about 1 inch. Using the prongs of a fork, lightly poke the bottom of the pie crust in several places. Par-bake the crust for 5 minutes; remove from the oven and allow to cool.

Increase oven temperature to 375° F.

In a skillet, heat the olive oil over medium heat. Once hot, add the mushrooms and sauté 2–3 minutes or until slightly softened. Add the asparagus, ¼ teaspoon salt, and ⅛ teaspoon pepper. Continue sautéing the vegetables an additional 6–8 minutes or until softened.

Meanwhile, whisk together the eggs, milk, and remaining ¼ teaspoon salt and ⅛ teaspoon pepper in a medium-sized bowl; set aside.

Once through cooking, layer half the cheese on the bottom of the par-baked crust. Transfer the sautéed vegetables on top of the cheese and top the vegetables with remaining cheese. Pour the egg mixture over the veggies. Bake the quiche 40– 45 minutes or until set. Allow to cool for 3–4 minutes before slicing and serving.

Yield: 6 slices

Nutrition Information (per slice):

411 calories; 33.3 g. fat; 229 mg. cholesterol; 479 mg. sodium; 11.9 g. carbohydrate; 5.2 g. fiber; 21.3 g. protein; 3.0 g. sugar

Cook's Comment:

You can use Swiss cheese in place of Gruyere for a very similar flavor or substitute in your favorite cheese. Or, omit the cheese altogether to reduce calories and saturated fat content.

Almond-Oat Strawberry and Banana Smoothie

½ cup gluten-free old-fashioned oats

8 oz. (about 8) fresh strawberries, stems removed

1 large banana, peeled

¼ cup almond flour

1½ cups unsweetened vanilla almond or coconut milk

1 cup ice

Directions:

Combine all ingredients in a blender and blend until smooth and ice is broken down. Serve immediately.

Yield: 32 ounces (4 servings; 1 cup each)

Nutrition Information (per cup):

130 calories; 5.5 g. fat; 0 mg. cholesterol; 70 mg. sodium; 18.8 g. carbohydrate; 4.0 g. fiber; 3.8 g. protein; 6.0 g. sugar

Nutrition Note:

Adding oats and almond flour to smoothies is a brilliant way to add fiber and stick-to-your-ribs goodness to keep you full for hours. The consistency becomes creamy, thick, and rich. You'll love it!

Chocolate-Cherry Biscotti

2 cups blanched almond flour

¼ cup unsweetened cocoa
  powder

2 tablespoons potato starch

1 teaspoon instant espresso
  powder

½ teaspoon Xanthan gum

¾ teaspoon salt

¾ teaspoon baking soda

⅓ cup cherries (about 10), pitted

¼ cup pure maple syrup

4 oz. 72% cacoa (or higher) dark
  chocolate

1 tablespoon almond slivers,
  crushed

Directions:

Preheat oven to 325° F. Line a baking sheet with parchment paper and set aside.

In a medium bowl, combine the almond flour, cocoa powder, potato starch, espresso powder, Xanthan gum, salt, and baking soda; set aside.

In the bowl of a food processor, purée fresh, pitted cherries. Measure out ¼ cup of the puree and set aside; remove any excess puree from the bowl of the food processor and return it to the motor base with the blade (no need to wash, rinse, or dry).

Add the almond flour mixture to the bowl of the food processor and pulse several times to combine well. To the bowl, add the cherry puree and the maple syrup. Pulse until the mixture becomes cohesive and moist, like Play-Doh.

Separate the dough into two equal pieces. Onto the parchment-lined baking sheet, form each piece of dough into "logs" that are approximately 6 inches long, 3–4 inches wide, and 1 inch thick. Bake for 25 minutes.

Remove biscotti from the oven and allow to cool.

Reduce oven temperature to 300° F.

Using a sharp serrated knife, cut the biscotti width-wise on a diagonal to make a total of 16 biscotti. Place the biscotti cut-side down onto the baking sheet and bake an additional 12–18 minutes or until dried out; remove from oven and allow to cool completely.

In a narrow, microwave-safe glass, melt the chocolate in the microwave on high, stirring every 15–20 seconds until

Cook's Comment:

Store gluten-free baked goods in the refrigerator for best results. The texture is best preserved this way.

Shopping Tip:

Not all dark chocolate is dairy-free and vegan. Be sure to read the ingredient list for milk and milk derivatives if you desire dairy-free and vegan chocolate.

melted. Tilt the glass and roll one end of each biscotti in the chocolate, shaking off any excess. Return to the baking sheet and top with crushed almond slivers. Repeat with remaining biscotti. Allow to cool completely before serving. Store refrigerated in an air-tight container.

Yield: 16 biscotti

Nutrition information (per biscotti):

155 calories; 10.6 g. fat; 0 mg. cholesterol; 113 mg. sodium; 13.0 g. carbohydrate; 2.9 g. fiber; 4.0 g. protein; 6.5 g. sugar

Peaches and Cream Steel-Cut Oats

4 cups unsweetened almond milk

2 cups water

1½ cups gluten-free steel-cut oats, uncooked

1 teaspoon vanilla extract

$1/3$ cup honey

1 peach, pitted and diced

$1/8$ teaspoon salt

½ cup almond flour

Directions:

In a large, nonstick sauce pan, bring the almond milk and water to a simmer over medium heat. Stir in the oats and cook 20 minutes or until slightly thickened, stirring every 5 minutes.

Stir in vanilla extract, honey, peach, salt, and almond flour; stir every 5 minutes, cooking an additional 15–20 minutes or until desired thickness.

Yield: 6 servings (about 1¼ cups each)

Nutrition Information (per serving):

317 calories; 9.7 g. fat; 0 mg. cholesterol; 174 mg. sodium; 50.2 g. carbohydrate; 7.0 g. fiber; 9.8 g. protein; 17.8 g. sugar

Cook's Comment:

Steel-cut oats are less processed than old-fashioned, quick, or instant oats and therefore take a bit longer to cook. However, their consistency is unique, hearty, and fun. For an effortless breakfast, try this recipe in the crock pot—combine all the ingredients in a crock pot, stir, and cook on low for 7–9 hours.

Nutrition Note:

Use agave or maple syrup to create a vegan version of this recipe!

Crepes with Raspberry Compote

Crepes:

5 eggs

1½ cups blanched almond flour

½ cup superfine brown rice flour

¼ teaspoon salt

1 tablespoon honey

½ teaspoon vanilla extract

1¼ cup unsweetened coconut or almond milk

Compote:

1½ cups raspberries

1 tablespoon honey

3 tablespoons water

1 tablespoon tapioca starch

Directions:

In a medium bowl, gently whisk the eggs. Whisk in the almond flour, brown rice flour, salt, honey, vanilla, and milk. Mixture should be thin and spread easily.

Preheat a large skillet over medium heat. Once hot, mist with cooking spray and pour a scant ½ cup of the mixture into the center of the skillet. Pick up the skillet and tilt in all directions to spread the batter into a 10-inch round crepe, working quickly. Cook the crepe for 2–3 minutes or until slightly browned; flip carefully and cook an additional 1–2 minutes. Repeat with remaining batter.

Meanwhile, combine the raspberries, honey, and water in a small sauce pan over medium heat. Cook for 8–10 minutes or until hot and bubbling. Whisk in the tapioca starch and cook for an additional 1–2 minutes to thicken.

Serve crepes with hot compote.

Yield: 4 servings, 2 crepes each with 2–3 tablespoons compote

Nutrition Information (per serving):

467 calories; 28.8 g. fat; 231 mg. cholesterol; 279 mg. sodium; 39.0 g. carbohydrate; 8.5 g. fiber; 18.8 g. protein; 12.0 g. sugar

Cook's Comment:

Invest in superfine brown rice flour, as it makes a world of difference in the texture of the end product. Most rice flours create very gritty textures, so it's important to bake with quality ingredients for quality results.

Banana Nut Waffles

3 cups blanched almond flour
1 teaspoon baking soda
½ teaspoon salt
7 oz. over-ripe bananas (about
　2 small)

4 eggs
1 teaspoon vanilla extract
½ cup unsalted walnuts,
　chopped

Directions:

Preheat a waffle iron.

In a large bowl, whisk together the almond flour, baking soda, and salt; set aside.

In a medium bowl, mash the peeled bananas against the side of the bowl using the back of a fork. Add the eggs and vanilla to the bananas and whisk to combine well.

Pour the banana-egg mixture into the almond flour mixture and combine well, until almond flour has absorbed the banana-egg mixture. Fold in the walnuts.

Cook the waffles according to manufacturer's directions, or about 2½ to 3½ minutes per waffle. Serve hot.

Yield: 5 servings

Nutrition Information (per serving):

542 calories; 44.2 g. fat; 148 mg. cholesterol; 551 mg. sodium; 25.0 g. carbohydrate; 8.8 g. fiber; 21.2 g. protein; 7.6 g. sugar

Nutrition Note:

Chock-full of heart-healthy fat and good-for-you calories, these Banana Nut Waffles are incredibly satisfying.

Baked Egg Cups

2 cups almond flour

¼ teaspoon salt

2 tablespoons unsalted butter,

cubed

13 eggs, divided

Cooking spray

Directions:

Preheat oven to 350° F. Mist a muffin tin with nonstick cooking spray.

In the bowl of a food processor, pulse together the almond flour and salt. Add the butter, cube by cube, pulsing between additions. Add one egg and pulse until you reach a crumb-like consistency.

Distribute the dough into each of 12 muffin wells, about 2–3 tablespoons per well. Using your fingers, work the dough into the bottom of the muffin wells and up the sides about 1 inch. Repeat with remaining dough. Bake the dough for 5 minutes and remove from oven.

Crack an egg into each muffin well and return to the oven to bake an additional 15–17 minutes. Yolks should be firm on the outside and soft on the inside. Serve hot.

Yield: 12 egg cups

Nutrition Information (per egg cup):

199 calories; 16.6 g. fat; 200 mg. cholesterol; 130 mg. sodium; 4.0 g. carbohydrate; 2.0 g. fiber; 10.5 g. protein; 0.7 g. sugar

Cook's Comment:

Does breakfast get any cuter than this? These are ultimate man and kid food alike! Get ready to please lots of people with this simple, classic, low-carb, gluten-free delight!

Honey-Almond Granola Clusters

2 cups gluten-free old-fashioned oats
$^1/_3$ cup almond flour
¼ teaspoon salt
$^1/_3$ cup almond slivers
$^1/_3$ cup dried cranberries
¼ cup honey
3 tablespoons extra-virgin olive oil
2 egg whites

Directions:

Preheat oven to 300° F. Line a baking sheet with parchment paper and set aside.

In a large bowl, combine the oats, almond flour, salt, almonds, and cranberries; toss well. To the bowl, add the honey and olive oil; mix well to coat mixture.

In a separate bowl, beat the egg whites until frothy white and tripled in size (soft peak stage). Fold the egg whites into the oat mixture.

Arrange the oats onto the baking sheet in a single layer. Bake for 40 minutes, stirring every 10 minutes. Once golden brown, remove from oven and allow to cool on the baking sheet. The clusters will firm up and become crunchy as they dry.

Yield: 3½ cups (7 servings; ½ cup each)

Nutrition Information (per ½ cup):

249 calories; 13.7 g. fat; 0 mg. cholesterol; 101 mg. sodium; 27.7 g. carbohydrate; 3.6 g. fiber; 6.3 g. protein; 11.1 g. sugar

Cook's Comment:

Egg whites are used to create crunchy granola that makes clusters of granola goodness. Be sure to stir the granola often as the edges tend to brown quickly.

Blueberry-Almond Breakfast Cake

2 cups blanched almond flour

2 teaspoons baking powder

½ teaspoon salt

1 cup fresh blueberries

4 large eggs

¼ cup unsweetened applesauce

2 tablespoons honey

Nutrition Note:

Subtly sweet, this breakfast cake is high in antioxidants from the blueberries and full of heart-healthy fats and fiber from the almond flour. Who says you can't have cake for breakfast?

Directions:

Preheat oven to 350° F. Mist a 10-inch spring-form pan with nonstick cooking spray; set aside.

In a large bowl, whisk to combine the almond flour, baking powder, and salt. Add the blueberries and gently mix.

In a separate bowl, whisk the eggs. Add the applesauce and honey and whisk to combine. Add the egg-applesauce mixture to the almond flour and mix to combine.

Transfer the batter to the spring-form pan and, using a spatula, spread the batter to the edges of the pan and smooth the top of the cake..

Bake the breakfast cake for 35–40 minutes or until top is slightly browned. Allow to cool for 10–15 minutes before running a knife along the sides of the spring-form pan and releasing to cut and serve.

Yield: 8 generous slices

Nutrition Information (per slice):

224 calories; 16.6 g. fat; 93 mg. cholesterol; 310 mg. sodium; 13.8 g. carbohydrate; 4.0 g. fiber; 9.4 g. protein; 6.6 g. sugar

Chocolate Donuts with Orange Glaze

Donuts:

1 cup sorghum flour
½ cup millet flour
½ cup potato starch
¼ cup blanched almond flour
¼ cup unsweetened cocoa
   powder
⅓ cup brown sugar, lightly
   packed
1 teaspoon baking powder
½ teaspoon baking soda
½ teaspoon salt
½ teaspoon Xanthan gum

¼ cup coconut oil, melted and
   cooled
½ cup 2% plain Greek yogurt
½ cup unsweetened vanilla
   almond milk
3 eggs, lightly beaten
1 teaspoon vanilla extract

Glaze:

3 tablespoons freshly squeezed
   orange juice
1½ cups powdered sugar

Cook's Comment:

Almond flour adds moisture to baked goods, while sorghum flour gives a slightly sweet quality to baked goods like donuts.

Directions:

Preheat oven to 350° F. Mist donut pan with nonstick cooking spray and set aside.

In a large bowl, whisk to combine the sorghum flour, millet flour, potato starch, almond flour, cocoa, brown sugar, baking powder, baking soda, salt, and Xanthan gum.

In a medium bowl, combine the coconut oil, yogurt, milk, eggs, and vanilla; beat well.

Add the wet ingredients to the dry, mixing well to combine.

Spoon batter into donut wells to fill about two-thirds full. Use wet fingers to smooth the tops of the batter slightly. Bake donuts for 15 minutes. Remove from oven and allow to cool 3–4 minutes; transfer warm donuts to a cooling rack to cool completely.

Meanwhile, combine the glaze ingredients in a shallow bowl, mixing until smooth. Once cooled completely, dunk the tops of each donut into the glaze and serve immediately.

Yield: 18 glazed donuts

Nutrition Information (per donut):

148 calories; 5.4 g. fat; 31 mg. cholesterol; 143 mg. sodium; 22.6 g. carbohydrate; 1.5 g. fiber; 3.5 g. protein; 9.1 g. sugar

Raw Fruit and Nut Truffles

1 cup (5.7 oz.) medjool dates, pitted
1 cup (6.8 oz.) dried apricots
½ cup (2 oz.) almond flour or meal
½ cup (1.2 oz.) unsweetened dried coconut
½ cup (2.8 oz.) dried cranberries
¼ cup (1.3 oz.) raw pistachios
½ cup (2 oz.) unsalted raw almonds
¼ cup (1.25 oz.) unsalted raw sunflower seeds

Directions:

In the bowl of a food processor, combine the dates, apricots, almond flour, coconut, and cranberries, processing until the mixture comes together in a single ball.

Add the pistachios, almonds, and sunflower seeds, pulsing to distribute well.

Roll the mixture into 1-inch balls. Refrigerate any leftover truffles.

Yield: 25 truffles

Nutrition Information (per truffle):

92 calories; 4.4 g. fat; 0 mg. cholesterol; 10 mg. sodium; 13.1 g. carbohydrate; 2.2 g. fiber; 2.9 g. protein; 9.8 g. sugar

Nutrition Note:

Nutritious foods are often calorically dense (small portions that are higher in calories). Don't let this deter you from consuming them, however! Foods such as nuts, seeds, and dried fruits are also nutrient dense and are nutritional powerhouses that offer lots of satiating power.

Protein Pancakes

1½ cups gluten-free oats
½ cup blanched almond flour
1 cup low-fat cottage cheese
1 teaspoon vanilla extract

4 eggs
1 teaspoon baking powder
2 tablespoons granulated sugar

Directions:

Combine all ingredients in a blender and blend until smooth. Allow batter to rest for 5 minutes.

Meanwhile, preheat a nonstick griddle to medium-high heat.

Using one-third cup measures, spoon the pancake batter onto the hot griddle and use the back of the measuring cup to spread batter to create a 6-inch, round pancake. Cook pancakes 3–4 minutes or until bubbles form all over the pancake surface; flip and cook an additional 1–2 minutes.

Serve pancakes hot with desired toppings.

Yield: 8 pancakes (4 servings, 2 pancakes each)

Nutrition Information (per serving):

330 calories; 15.3 g. fat; 193 mg. cholesterol; 425 mg. sodium; 31.8 g. carbohydrate; 5.0 g. fiber; 18.8 g. protein; 8.8 g. sugar

Cook's Comment:

Breakfast … fast! It doesn't get much easier than throwing everything into a blender and letting it do the work. You'll be pleased with how well these pancakes heat up as leftovers, too! Double batch, anyone?

Toasted Coconut and Peach Breakfast Crumble

5 large peaches (about 2 lbs),
   pitted and roughly chopped
½ cup unsweetened coconut
   flakes
¼ cup tapioca starch

1 cup gluten-free rolled oats
½ cup almond flour
¼ teaspoon salt
2 tablespoons coconut oil
2 tablespoons honey

Directions:

Preheat oven to 350° F. Mist an 8 x 8-in baking dish with nonstick cooking spray and set aside.

Arrange the coconut flakes on a baking sheet and bake for 4–6 minutes or until beginning to brown; remove and allow to cool.

In a medium bowl, combine the peaches and tapioca starch; toss to coat. Add the coconut and mix well. Transfer the peaches and coconut to the 8-inch baking dish.

In the bowl of a mini food prep, food chopper, or food processor, combine the oats, almond flour, salt, coconut oil, and honey. Pulse 10–20 times, or until the mixture is moist and crumbly. Using your fingers, crumble the oat mixture evenly over top of the peaches and bake for 35–40 minutes or until the top of the crumble turns golden and the peaches are softened. Serve warm.

Yield: 4 large servings

Nutrition Information (per serving):

418 calories; 22.0 g. fat; 0 mg. cholesterol; 149 mg. sodium; 53.5 g. carbohydrate; 8.5 g. fiber; 7.3 g. protein; 26.3 g. sugar

Cook's Comment:

Peaches and coconut are made for one another. This breakfast crumble could easily double as dessert.

Nutrition Note:

Use agave or maple syrup to create a vegan version of this recipe!

Tropical Fruit and Coconut Scones

1 cup sorghum flour
¾ cup blanched almond flour
½ cup tapioca starch
2 teaspoons baking powder
½ teaspoon baking soda
½ teaspoon salt
1 teaspoon Xanthan gum
3 tablespoons granulated sugar
5 tablespoons coconut oil, solid

2 eggs
¼ cup unsweetened applesauce
2 teaspoons pure vanilla extract
⅓ cup fresh pineapple, finely diced
⅓ cup fresh mango, finely diced
⅓ cup unsweetened coconut flakes

Directions:

Preheat oven to 350° F. Line a baking sheet with parchment paper and set aside.

In a large bowl, whisk to combine the sorghum flour, almond flour, tapioca starch, baking powder, baking soda, salt, Xanthan gum, and sugar. Drop the coconut oil into well-mixed dry ingredients and cut in the solid oil using the back of a fork or pastry cutter until the fat is well dispersed and the dry ingredients form in small clumps.

In a medium bowl, whisk together the eggs, applesauce, and vanilla. Mix the wet ingredients into the dry until incorporated. Fold in the pineapple, mango, and coconut, mixing well.

Turn the dough out onto a nonstick flat surface, such as a piece of parchment or wax paper on a countertop, and flatten into a 9- or 10-inch round, about 1 to 1½ inches thick. Cut scones into 8 wedges and carefully transfer the scones to the parchment-lined baking sheet, spacing them at least 2 inches apart.

Bake scones for 20–25 minutes or until slightly golden brown.

Yield: 8 scones

Nutrition Information (per scone):

290 calories; 17.8 g. fat; 46 mg. cholesterol; 361 mg. sodium; 30.0 g. carbohydrate; 3.9 g. fiber; 5.8 g. protein; 6.5 g. sugar

Nutrition Note:

Who says scones need butter? Myth! Coconut oil is very high in saturated fat, but unlike other oils, it is made primarily of medium-chain triglycerides. This type of fat is processed very differently in the body and may not pose the same atherosclerotic risk as other saturated fats. Plus, the flavor is unbeatable.

Cranberry and Chocolate Chip Breakfast Bars

3 cups gluten-free oats
1 cup almond flour
⅓ cup walnuts, chopped
½ cup whole almonds
½ cup dried cranberries
¼ cup unsalted sunflower seeds

½ teaspoon salt
⅓ cup mini chocolate chips
½ cup honey
½ cup coconut oil, melted and
  cooled
1 egg

Directions:

Preheat oven to 350° F.

Spread oats on a baking sheet and bake for 6–8 minutes, stirring once. Remove and allow to cool.

Meanwhile, combine almond flour, walnuts, almonds, cranberries, sunflower seeds, salt, and chocolate chips in a large bowl. Add cooled oats and stir.

In a medium bowl, combine the honey, coconut oil, and egg, whisking well to combine.

Stir the wet ingredients into the dry oat mixture and mix well, distributing the honey mixture evenly throughout. Transfer the mixture to a 9- x 13-inch baking dish that has been lined with parchment paper. Use the back of a spatula misted with nonstick cooking spray to flatten the mixture evenly and firmly in the bottom of the dish to create an even layer.

Bake the breakfast bars for 20–25 minutes or until just beginning to turn golden. Remove from oven and allow to cool completely. Cut bars and store in an air-tight container or wrap individually in foil to freeze.

Yield: 12 breakfast bars

Nutrition Information (per bar):

337 calories; 21.7 g. fat; 15 mg. cholesterol; 124 mg. sodium; 32.8 g. carbohydrate; 4.5 g. fiber; 7.0 g. protein; 15.9 g. sugar

Cook's Comment:

Breakfast bars are a blank slate. Add or subtract ingredients, as you prefer. There's really no going wrong! The almond flour in this recipe not only adds nutrition, but also acts as a glue to keep the bars from crumbling after baking.

Sides, Starters, and Accompaniments

Sweet and Savory Bacon-Wrapped Jalapeño Poppers

7 jalapeños, halved lengthwise, seeded and ribs removed

4 oz. reduced-fat cream cheese, softened

¼ cup (1 oz.) part-skim cheddar cheese, shredded

3 tablespoons brown sugar

3 tablespoons almond flour

½ teaspoon chili powder

¼ teaspoon smoked paprika

¼ teaspoon cumin

¼ teaspoon salt

7 pieces uncured turkey bacon, halved length-wise

Directions:

Preheat oven to 350° F. Fit a wire cooling rack over a baking sheet and set aside.

In a small bowl, combine the cream cheese and cheddar cheese, mixing well.

In a shallow bowl, combine the brown sugar, almond flour, chili powder, paprika, cumin, and salt; mix well.

One at a time, stuff each jalapeño with the cream cheese mixture, wrap with a piece of bacon, and gently roll into the brown sugar mixture. Arrange the poppers on the wire rack and repeat with remaining poppers.

Bake poppers 20–22 minutes or until bacon is cooked through and cheese is hot. Allow poppers to cool several minutes before serving.

Yield: 14 poppers.

Nutrition information (per popper):

57 calories; 4.0 g. fat; 12 mg. cholesterol; 152 mg. sodium; 2.6 g. carbohydrate;
0.4 g. fiber; 2.4 g. protein; 2.4 g. sugar

Nutrition Note:

Much lighter than fried versions, this sweet and spicy rendition is sure to please. Unlike most jalapeño poppers, some of the fat in this recipe is from heart-healthy almonds.

Green Beans Amandine

1 lb fresh green beans, trimmed

Juice of ½ lemon

1 tablespoon olive oil

¼ cup blanched almond flour

¼ teaspoon salt

⅛ teaspoon pepper

¼ cup almond slivers

Directions:

Preheat oven to 400° F.

In a large sauce pan, bring 2–3 quarts of water to a rolling boil over high heat. Once boiling, add the green beans. Cook about 6–8 minutes, or until bright green and slightly tender. Drain the beans through a colander and return them to the pan.

Add lemon juice and olive oil to the pan and toss well to coat; drain any excess liquid before proceeding.

Add the almond flour, salt, pepper, and almond slivers; toss and transfer the beans to a 2-quart baking dish.

Bake the beans for 8–12 minutes, depending on texture preference. Serve hot.

Yield: 5 side servings (about ¾ cup each)

Nutrition Information (per serving):

122 calories; 8.4 g. fat; 0 mg. cholesterol; 123 mg. sodium; 9.2 g. carbohydrate; 4.4 g. fiber; 4.0 g. protein; 1.8 g. sugar

Cook's Comment:

Adding texture to vegetable dishes is what can make them seem like something more than just that . . . vegetables. Experiment with textures in your veggie dishes to make them more enticing and lure people to seconds!

Parmesan Zucchini Sticks with Feta Romesco Dipping Sauce

Zucchini:
4 small zucchini (1 lb), cut into
    ¾-inch thick sticks
1 teaspoon olive oil
¾ cup almond flour
¼ cup grated Parmesan cheese
1 teaspoon Italian seasoning
½ teaspoon salt
3 eggs, lightly beaten
2 tablespoons brown rice flour
Olive oil cooking spray

Dipping Sauce:
2 Roma tomatoes, quartered
12 oz. jar roasted red peppers,
    drained
2 oz. feta cheese
2 garlic cloves, peeled
1 tablespoon blanched almond
    flour
Black pepper, to taste

Fun Fact:

This Feta-Romesco sauce can double as a pasta sauce. Grab your favorite gluten-free pasta and turn leftover appetizers into dinner or vice versa.

Directions:

Preheat oven to 400° F. Line a baking sheet with parchment paper and set aside.

In a small sauce pan, heat olive oil over medium heat. Once hot, add ¾ cup almond flour and stir. Cook flour 6–8 minutes, stirring frequently. Once browned, remove from heat and transfer to a shallow bowl to cool. Stir in Parmesan cheese, Italian seasoning, and salt.

In a second shallow bowl, lightly beat the eggs and whisk in the brown rice flour.

In a mini food prep or food processor, combine all of the dipping sauce ingredients. Transfer dipping sauce to the pan used to cook the almond flour and bring to a simmer over medium heat, stirring occasionally. The mixture will thicken as it cooks.

Working one at a time, dip the zucchini stick quarters into the egg mixture, followed by the almond flour and cheese mixture, carefully coating and transferring them to the baking sheet. Mist zucchini sticks with olive oil and bake for 20 minutes. Serve with warm Feta Romesco Dipping Sauce.

Yield: 8 appetizer servings (2 sticks with 2 tablespoons romesco each)

Nutrition Information (per serving):

156 calories; 10.6 g. fat; 72 mg. cholesterol; 347 mg. sodium; 7.3 g. carbohydrate; 2.8 g. fiber; 7.9 g. protein; 2.3 g. sugar

Tossed Greens with Honey-Almond Vinaigrette

2 tablespoons almond flour
¼ cup extra-virgin olive oil
¼ cup honey
2 tablespoons white wine
   vinegar

1 teaspoon Dijon mustard
⅛ teaspoon salt
Black pepper, to taste
8 oz. salad greens

Directions:

In a small blender or mini food processor, combine the almond flour, olive oil, honey, vinegar, mustard, salt, and pepper. Blend until well combined.

Place salad greens in a large bowl and drizzle with dressing; toss well and serve immediately.

Yield: 6 servings

Nutrition Information (per serving):

157 calories; 10.2 g. fat; 0 mg. cholesterol; 140 mg. sodium; 16.0 g. carbohydrate; 2.3 g. fiber; 2.5 g. protein; 11.7 g. sugar

Cook's Comment:

When you process almond flour as vinaigrette, the result is creamy and rich. Who knew almond flour could be *this* versatile?

Lump Crab Cakes with Lemon Pepper Aioli

Crab Cakes:

10 oz. lump crabmeat

2 green onions, sliced

¼ cup green bell pepper, minced

¼ teaspoon black pepper

2 tablespoons low-fat olive oil–based mayonnaise

1 egg

½ cup almond flour

1 tablespoon olive oil

Aioli:

2 tablespoons low-fat olive oil–based mayonnaise

2 tablespoons nonfat plain Greek yogurt

Juice of ½ lemon

½ teaspoon lemon pepper

¼ teaspoon salt

Cook's Comment:

If the crab cakes are too moist to easily form into cakes, add a few tablespoons of additional almond flour and try again. The consistency will be slightly wet and sticky, but you should be able to form the mixture into cakes.

Directions:

In a medium bowl, combine the crab, green onion, bell pepper, black pepper, mayonnaise, egg, and almond flour; mix well.

In a large skillet over medium-high heat, heat the olive oil until rippling and hot. Using your hands, form the crab mixture into 3-inch patties, about 1 inch thick. The mixture will be very moist, but should be able to be formed into a patty. Drop the crab cakes into the hot skillet, one by one. Cook 3–4 minutes or until golden; carefully flip the cakes and cook an additional 2–3 minutes. Remove the crab cakes to a paper towel–lined plate to absorb excess oil.

Meanwhile, combine the aioli ingredients in a small dish. Serve the crab cakes hot with aioli.

Yield: 6 crab cakes

Nutrition Information (per crab cake with 2 teaspoons aioli):

149 calories; 10.2 g. fat; 72 mg. cholesterol; 359 mg. sodium; 4.0 g. carbohydrate; 1.3 g. fiber; 11.8 g. protein; 0.8 g. sugar

Cheese and Herb-Roasted Fingerling Potatoes

2 lbs fingerling potatoes, halved lengthwise

3 tablespoons extra-virgin olive oil

½ teaspoon + ⅛ teaspoon salt, divided

¼ teaspoon black pepper

4 teaspoons fresh herbs (i.e., oregano, rosemary, thyme), minced and divided

¼ cup almond flour

1 oz. Pecorino cheese, grated

Directions:

Preheat oven to 375° F. Arrange a wire baking rack over a baking sheet and mist with cooking spray; set aside.

In a large bowl, combine the potatoes and olive oil; toss well to coat. Sprinkle potatoes with ½ teaspoon salt, ¼ teaspoon black pepper, and 3 teaspoons fresh herbs; toss well. Arrange potatoes in a single layer on the baking sheet and bake for 40 minutes.

Meanwhile, combine the almond flour, Pecorino, and remaining teaspoon herbs; mix.

After 40 minutes, remove potatoes from oven and sprinkle almond flour-cheese mixture evenly over the tops of the potatoes. Return potatoes to oven and bake an additional 5 minutes. Remove potatoes from oven, toss, and serve hot.

Yield: 6 servings

Nutrition Information (per serving):

200 calories; 10.5 g. fat; 4 mg. cholesterol; 325 mg. sodium; 21.3 g. carbohydrate; 2.2 g. fiber; 5.0 g. protein; 0.2 g. sugar

Cook's Comment:

If you prefer, use an alternate type of potato in this recipe. Even sweet potatoes would be a fun adaptation to create a sweet and savory combination.

Almond and Herb-Stuffed Artichokes

2 large artichokes, trimmed and stem chopped off
¼ cup almond flour
2 tablespoons grated Parmesan cheese
¹/₈ teaspoon salt
¹/₈ teaspoon pepper
2 tablespoons fresh parsley, minced

1 tablespoon fresh rosemary, minced
1 lemon, juiced and divided
1 tablespoon extra-virgin olive oil
1–2 quarts boiling water

Directions:

Preheat oven to 425° F.

Trim the tops of the artichoke leaves by chopping off the top ½ inch, as well as individually trimming the leaves closer to the stem of the vegetable. Carefully loosen the leaves of the artichoke by separating leaves from others, making space for the stuffing.

In a small bowl, combine the almond flour, Parmesan, salt, pepper, parsley, and rosemary; mix well. Add half the lemon juice and stir to combine. Sprinkle the mixture over the artichoke, distributing between the layers of leaves. Transfer artichokes to a baking dish, standing upright, and drizzle with remaining lemon juice and the olive oil.

Carefully fill the baking dish with 1 inch of water, surrounding the bases of the artichokes with water. Cover the baking dish tightly with foil and bake for 1 hour, or until outer leaves are tender. Serve hot.

Yield: 2 servings

Nutrition Information (per serving):

233 calories; 16.0 g. fat; 5 mg. cholesterol; 277 mg. sodium; 18.5 g. carbohydrate; 8.5 g. fiber; 9.0 g. protein; 1.0 g. sugar

Shopping Tip:

Look for artichokes starting in March when they come into season. Their season runs through May. Much different in texture than their canned varieties, the hearts are meaty and firm. As you peel off the individual leaves to nibble off the tip of artichoke meat, you slowly approach the heart of the artichoke like the hidden gem that it is.

Coconut Shrimp with Pineapple Dipping Sauce

Dipping Sauce:
8 oz. pineapple, finely diced
1 cup lite coconut milk (canned)
¼ cup coconut rum
$^1/_3$ cup sweetened coconut flakes
2 tablespoons powdered sugar

Shrimp:
1 lb large shrimp, peeled and
    deveined, tails on
1 tablespoon tapioca starch

½ cup lite coconut milk
    (canned)
½ cup almond flour
$^1/_3$ cup unsweetened coconut
    flakes
$^1/_3$ cup sweetened coconut
    flakes
1 tablespoon powdered sugar
$^1/_8$ teaspoon salt

Cook's Comment:

Keep an eye on the shrimp as they bake—coconut flakes have a tendency to burn easily. Consider using a middle or bottom rack in the oven, as well.

Directions:

In a small sauce pan, combine the pineapple, coconut milk, rum, coconut flakes, and powdered sugar for the pineapple dipping sauce. Set the pan over medium-high heat and bring to a boil. Reduce heat and allow it to simmer and reduce for 10–15 minutes. Remove sauce from heat and bring to room temperature. Refrigerate until well-chilled.

Preheat oven to 375° F.

Pat shrimp dry using a paper towel or clean cloth and transfer to a medium bowl. Sprinkle with tapioca starch and toss to coat shrimp evenly.

In one bowl, pour ½ cup coconut milk. In a second bowl, combine the almond flour, coconut flakes (unsweetened and sweetened), powdered sugar, and salt; toss well.

One at a time, holding the shrimp by the tail, dredge through the coconut milk, shaking off any excess, and then carefully roll the shrimp in the almond flour and coconut mixture; shake off any excess. Arrange the shrimp on a baking sheet and repeat with remaining shrimp, working one at a time.

Bake shrimp 11–13 minutes. Serve alongside the pineapple dipping sauce.

Yield: 24 shrimp with dipping sauce (8 servings; 3 shrimp each)

Nutrition Information (per serving):

227 calories; 10.9 g. fat; 75 mg. cholesterol; 146 mg. sodium; 15.1 g. carbohydrate; 2.0 g. fiber; 13.5 g. protein; 7.5 g. sugar

Entrées

Eggplant Parmigana

1 medium eggplant, sliced into
    12 slices
2 eggs, lightly beaten
¾ cup almond flour
¾ cup gluten-free rice krispies,
    crushed to coarse crumbs
1 teaspoon garlic powder
¼ teaspoon salt
¼ teaspoon black pepper
½ cup low-fat ricotta
3 tablespoons fresh basil,
    minced

2 oz. Parmigiano Reggiano,
    grated and divided
1 clove garlic, minced
¼ to ½ teaspoon crushed red
    pepper
1¼ cup gluten-free jarred
    marinara sauce
3 oz. fresh mozzarella, thinly
    sliced into 6 slices

Fun Fact:

Honestly, eggplant isn't my most favorite food . . . but these eggplant stacks will change anyone's mind about eggplant. There's nothing not to love about this dish, including its classy, fun presentation.

Directions:

Preheat oven to 375° F. Arrange a wire baking rack over a baking sheet and mist with cooking spray; set aside.

Set up a dredging station with beaten eggs in one shallow bowl, and in a second bowl, combine the almond flour, crushed rice krispies, garlic powder, salt, and pepper. Dip each slice of eggplant first in the egg and then into the almond flour-rice krispie mixture, shaking off any excess. Transfer the breaded eggplant to the wire baking rack and repeat with remaining eggplant. Reserve excess egg mixture and bake eggplant for 30 minutes or until slightly golden; remove from oven.

Meanwhile, to the reserved eggs, add the ricotta, basil, half of the Parmigiano Reggiano, garlic, and crushed red pepper; mix well.

In a 9 x 13-inch baking dish, spread ½ cup of the marinara on the bottom to coat. Arrange 6 of the eggplant slices atop the marinara. Top each eggplant slice with 1 tablespoon marinara followed by 2 tablespoons of the ricotta mixture, a slice of mozzarella, a second slice of eggplant, and finally, an additional tablespoon of marinara. Sprinkle each eggplant stack with a bit of the remaining Parmigiano Reggiano. Bake eggplant stacks for 10-15 minutes or until cheese is bubbly and hot. Serve immediately.

Yield: 3 servings (2 eggplant stacks each)

Nutrition Information (per serving):

525 calories; 31.7 g. fat; 173 mg. cholesterol; 704 mg. sodium; 35.7 g. carbohydrate; 8.7 g. fiber; 30.7 g. protein; 18.7 g. sugar

Almond-Crusted Fish Nuggets with Chipotle Tartar Sauce

Fish Nuggets:
1 lb cod, cut into 2-inch pieces
1¼ cup almond flour
½ teaspoon cumin
1 teaspoon dried oregano
¼ teaspoon salt
¼ teaspoon pepper
2 eggs

Tartar Sauce:
⅓ cup nonfat plain Greek yogurt
3 tablespoons low-fat olive
    oil-based
    mayonnaise
1–2 chipotles in adobo, minced
2 teaspoons pickle relish
¼ teaspoon salt

Cook's Comment:

A little cumin in the almond flour coating and super spicy chipotles in adobo kick this recipe up a notch with both flavor and spice!

Directions:

Preheat oven to 375° F. Place a wire cooling rack over a baking sheet and mist with nonstick cooking spray; set aside.

In a medium skillet over medium-low heat, toast the almond flour until it just begins to brown and becomes fragrant. Remove from heat and transfer to a shallow bowl. To the almond flour, add the cumin, oregano, salt, and pepper.

In a second shallow bowl, whisk the eggs.

Dunk each fish nugget into the egg and then carefully roll in the almond flour; transfer to the wire rack. Repeat with remaining fish nuggets. Bake fish for 11–13 minutes or until cooked through.

Meanwhile, combine the tartar sauce ingredients in a small bowl. Serve the hot fish nuggets with tartar sauce.

Yield: 4 servings (4 ounces fish with 2–3 tablespoons tartar sauce)

Nutrition Information (per serving):

314 calories; 19.0 g. fat; 99 mg. cholesterol; 557 mg. sodium; 8.5 g. carbohydrate; 3.3 g. fiber; 30.0 g. protein; 2.5 g. sugar

Pan-Fried Chicken Breasts with White Balsamic Peaches

Chicken:

1 lb boneless, skinless chicken
   breasts
   (about 4 breasts)
1 egg, lightly beaten
¾ cup almond flour
½ teaspoon salt
¼ teaspoon pepper
2 tablespoons extra-virgin
   olive oil

Peaches:

1 tablespoon coconut oil
1 teaspoon fresh rosemary,
   minced
2 peaches, pitted and sliced
2 tablespoons white balsamic
   vinegar
1 tablespoon brown sugar

Cook's Comment:

This recipe can be ready in less than 20 minutes, making it perfect for fast, weeknight cooking.

Directions:

Place the lightly beaten egg in one shallow dish and, in a second shallow dish, combine the almond flour, salt, and pepper. Dredge the chicken in the egg followed by the almond flour, coating both sides well; shake off excess flour.

Heat the olive oil in a large skillet over medium-high heat. Once hot, add the chicken and cook 5–6 minutes per side, or until golden brown and cooked through.

Meanwhile, melt the coconut oil in a medium skillet over high heat. Add the rosemary and cook until fragrant, stirring constantly, about 30 seconds. Add the peaches, vinegar, and brown sugar, stir, and bring to a simmer. Once simmering, reduce heat to medium and allow to cook 6–7 minutes or until peaches are softened and vinegar becomes syrupy.

Serve hot peaches and sauce over each of the chicken breasts.

Yield: 4 servings

Nutrition Information (per serving):

389 calories; 22.5 g. fat; 101 mg. cholesterol; 353 mg. sodium; 16.5 g. carbohydrate; 3.5 g. fiber; 32.8 g. protein; 11.8 g. sugar

Roasted Tofu and Vegetables in Spicy Peanut Sauce

Tofu and Vegetables:

2 large eggs

½ cup blanched almond flour

¼ cup unsweetened almond milk

¼ to ½ teaspoon crushed red pepper

14 oz. extra-firm tofu, cut into bite-size cubes

¼ teaspoon salt

¼ teaspoon black pepper

12 oz. fresh broccoli, cut into florets

8 oz. fresh snap peas

Peanut Sauce:

⅓ cup natural peanut butter

Juice of 1 lime

3 tablespoons low-sodium soy sauce

1 tablespoon toasted sesame oil

2 tablespoons extra-virgin olive oil

½ teaspoon crushed red pepper, or more to taste

Water to thin, as needed

Shopping Tip

Buying unsalted nuts helps keep sodium levels under control. Salted nuts typically contain more than 100 milligrams of unnecessary sodium per serving. You can always add salt, if desired.

Directions:

Preheat oven to 425° F. Line two baking sheets with parchment paper and set aside.

In a medium bowl, lightly beat the eggs. Add almond flour, milk, and crushed red pepper, and whisk to combine into a batter. Add the tofu into the batter and gently toss. One at a time, remove the tofu pieces to one of the baking sheets, allowing excess batter to drip off. Once tofu is arranged on the baking sheet, sprinkle with the salt and pepper.

On the second baking sheet, arrange the broccoli and snap peas.

Bake both the tofu and vegetables for 20–25 minutes, flipping the tofu halfway through baking.

Meanwhile, combine the ingredients for the peanut sauce in a small bowl, whisking well. Add additional crushed red pepper, to taste, and water to thin the sauce, if desired.

After roasting, combine the tofu and broccoli in a large bowl. Drizzle the peanut sauce over the top and gently toss to distribute the peanut sauce over the mixture. Serve immediately over hot rice, if desired.

Yield: 5 servings (about 1¼ cups each)

Nutrition Information (per serving):

371 calories; 26.8 g. fat; 56 mg. cholesterol; 563 mg. sodium; 15.0 g. carbohydrate; 5.4 g. fiber; 18.6 g. protein; 3.2 g. sugar

Spinach and Feta Chicken Rollatini

2 teaspoons olive oil, divided
⅔ cup almond flour
2 tablespoons grated Parmesan
4 oz. fresh spinach
2 sundried tomatoes packed in
    olive oil, drained and chopped
1 oz. feta, crumbled

1 egg
⅛ teaspoon salt and black
    pepper, to taste
14 oz. boneless, skinless chicken
    breasts (about 3 breasts),
    pounded to ¼- to
    ½-inch thickness

Directions:

Preheat oven to 400° F. Line a baking sheet with parchment or foil and set aside.

Heat 1 teaspoon of the oil in a skillet over medium heat. Once hot, add the almond flour and stir to distribute oil through flour. Brown the almond flour for 4–5 minutes, stirring often to avoid burning. Once browned, move to a shallow bowl and allow to cool. Add Parmesan and stir well; set aside.

Heat the remaining teaspoon of oil in the same skillet over medium heat. Add the spinach and cook to wilt, about 2–3 minutes, stirring often. Add the sun-dried tomatoes and stir. Remove from heat and stir in the feta.

In a shallow bowl, whisk together the egg, salt, and pepper.

Arrange one-third of the spinach mixture onto each pounded chicken breast; lightly press to help hold together. Roll the chicken breasts, starting at one end. Carefully dip chicken into egg and rotate to coat. Next, roll the chicken in the almond flour mixture and arrange on baking sheet.

Bake for 20–25 minutes or until chicken is cooked through. Serve hot.

Yield: 3 servings

Nutrition Information (per serving):

384 calories; 20.7 g. fat; 129 mg. cholesterol; 383 mg. sodium; 8.7 g. carbohydrate; 4.0 g. fiber; 41.0 g. protein; 2.3 g. sugar

Cook's Comment:

Bold flavors and an appealing presentation can take plain old chicken breasts to exciting, healthy new places. Enjoy!

Ricotta-Basil Turkey Meatballs

20 oz. ground turkey breast

1 egg

¼ cup almond flour

¼ cup low-fat ricotta cheese

2 cloves garlic, minced

2 tablespoons basil, minced

½ teaspoon crushed red pepper

½ teaspoon salt

¼ teaspoon black pepper

1 tablespoon extra-virgin olive oil

24 oz. gluten-free spaghetti sauce

Directions:

Combine turkey, egg, almond flour, ricotta, garlic, basil, crushed red pepper, salt, and pepper in a medium bowl. Combine mixture well, avoiding over-mixing. Roll the meat mixture into 20 balls, roughly 1 ounce each.

Heat olive oil in a large skillet over medium heat. Once hot, add the meatballs and cook 2–3 minutes before turning onto an opposite side. Cook an additional 2–3 minutes and turn meatballs again. Add the spaghetti sauce to the pan and cover loosely with a lid, stirring every 2–3 minutes.

Allow meatballs to simmer in the spaghetti sauce for 10–12 minutes or until heated through and cooked completely. Serve hot over gluten-free pasta with additional spaghetti sauce, if desired.

Yield: 5 servings (4 meatballs each)

Nutrition Information (per serving):

264 calories; 10.0 g. fat; 86 mg. cholesterol; 682 mg. sodium; 13.0 g. carbohydrate; 1.8 g. fiber; 32.2 g. protein; 6.6 g. sugar

Cook's Comment

Both ricotta and almond flour add moisture to these meatballs. Turkey breast can certainly end up tough and dry, but not in this recipe.

Sesame and Almond-Crusted Salmon with Cilantro Chimichurri

Salmon:

1 lb skinless salmon filets (4 filets)

2 teaspoons extra-virgin olive oil

¼ cup almond flour

½ tablespoon poppyseeds

1 tablespoon sesame seeds

¼ teaspoon salt

⅛ teaspoon black pepper

Chimichurri:

1 cup cilantro, lightly packed

Juice of ½ lime

¼ teaspoon salt

⅛ teaspoon black pepper

2 cloves garlic

¼ cup extra-virgin olive oil

Nutrition Note:

Chimichurri sauces are not only a stunning addition to proteins, but they're also full of nutrients. Herbs and olive oil are packed with antioxidants and fiber.

Directions:

Preheat oven to 375° F.

Brush both sides of the filets with olive oil and set aside.

In a shallow bowl, combine the almond flour, poppyseeds, sesame seeds, salt, and pepper; mix well. Dredge each side of the filet into the almond flour mixture and transfer to a baking sheet that has been misted with olive oil. Repeat with remaining filets.

Bake salmon filets for 15–20 minutes or until flesh is no longer opaque.

Meanwhile, combine chimichurri ingredients in the bowl of a mini food processor, food prep, or blender, and pulse to combine well and to desired consistency.

Serve salmon hot with chimichurri drizzled over the top.

Yield: 4 servings (4 oz. filet with 1½ tablespoons chimichurri)

Nutrition Information (per serving):

419 calories; 29.5 g. fat; 67 mg. cholesterol; 359 mg. sodium; 3.3 g. carbohydrate; 1.0 g. fiber; 31.3 g. protein; 0.3 g. sugar

Spicy Quinoa and Pinto Bean Burgers

½ cup dry quinoa

1 teaspoon extra-virgin olive oil

¼ red onion, minced

½ teaspoon salt, divided

2 cloves garlic, minced

1 (15 oz.) can pinto beans, drained and rinsed

2 tablespoons tomato paste

1 egg, lightly beaten

⅔ cup frozen corn

¼ cup almond flour

½ cup gluten-free oats

½ cup cilantro, minced

1–2 chipotles in adobo, minced

2 teaspoons ground cumin

½ teaspoon chipotle chile powder

Cook's Comment

To make this recipe vegan, replace the egg with a "flax egg." Simply combine 1 tablespoon flax meal or ground flaxseed with 3 tablespoons water and combine well. Allow the mixture to sit in the refrigerator for about 10 minutes before using, giving it time to gelatinize and create a strong binder for cooking and baking.

Directions:

Cook quinoa according to package directions, omitting salt and fat; set aside.

Meanwhile, heat olive oil in a small skillet until hot. Add the onion and season with ¼ teaspoon salt. Sauté onion 4–5 minutes, stirring occasionally, until softened. To the onions, add the garlic and sauté 30–60 seconds or until fragrant. Remove from heat and transfer onions to a large bowl.

To the onions, add the beans. Using a potato masher or the back of a fork, mash the beans until a paste-like consistency is achieved. Mix in remaining ingredients, including remaining ¼ teaspoon salt, and fold in the cooked quinoa.

Form the quinoa-bean mixture into 6 burger patties, each about 4 inches in diameter and ½-inch thick. Refrigerate for at least 1 hour or overnight.

Preheat grill to medium-high heat. Grill the burgers for 5–6 minutes per side on either an electric grill or outdoor grill. Serve on a gluten-free bun with your favorite toppings.

Yield: 6 burger patties

Nutrition Information (per patty):

217 calories; 5.8 g. fat; 31 mg. cholesterol; 371 mg. sodium; 34.8 g. carbohydrate; 7.2 g. fiber; 9.5 g. protein; 3.7 g. sugar

Pasta with Scallops and Creamy Lemon Goat Cheese

8 oz. dry corn pasta or gluten-free pasta of choice

¼ cup + 2 teaspoons extra-virgin olive oil, divided

1 bunch kale, ribs removed and roughly chopped

½ cup almond flour

1 tablespoon unsalted butter

12 oz. scallops

4 oz. goat cheese, softened

Juice of 1 lemon

2 cloves garlic

½ teaspoon salt

¼ teaspoon black pepper

Directions:

Bring 2–3 quarts of water to a rolling boil over medium-high heat. Add the pasta, stir, and allow to cook for 9–12 minutes or until al dente. Drain and keep hot.

Meanwhile, heat 1 teaspoon of the oil in a large skillet. Add the kale and sauté 2–3 minutes or until warm and wilted; remove to a plate.

In the same skillet, add another teaspoon of oil, swirling to coat the pan. Add the almond flour and toast it over medium heat, stirring occasionally until slightly browned, about 3–4 minutes. Remove flour to a small bowl.

Wipe the skillet with a dry cloth and return to the stovetop. Increase the heat to high and add the butter. Once hot, add the scallops and cook 2–3 minutes per side.

While cooking, blend the remaining ¼ cup olive oil, goat cheese, lemon juice, garlic, salt, and pepper in a mini food processor or blender until smooth and whipped.

Transfer the hot pasta to a large bowl and toss with goat cheese mixture to coat. Add in the kale and almond flour; toss well. Serve the pasta hot and topped with scallops.

Yield: 4 servings (about 1 cup pasta with 3–4 scallops)

Nutrition Information (per serving):

619 calories; 33.5 g. fat; 37 mg. cholesterol; 561 mg. sodium; 58.3 g. carbohydrate; 5.0 g. fiber; 26.8 g. protein; 1.8 g. sugar

Nutrition Note:

If kale isn't your favorite leafy green vegetable, swap in collard greens, mustard greens, or spinach. Sneaking leafy greens into pasta recipes is a great way to make a complete meal out of one dish, add nutrition, and stretch high-calorie ingredients such as cheese and butter.

Chile Rellenos

Salsa

3 large tomatoes, quartered
3 cloves garlic
¼ teaspoon salt
2 tablespoons fresh lime juice
1 jalapeno, seeds and ribs
   removed
1 chipotle in adobo
¼ cup red onion
¼ cup cilantro, lightly packed
1 teaspoon cumin

Chiles

8 poblano peppers
8 oz queso fresco, sliced into 1
   ounce pieces
6 eggs
¼ teaspoon salt
¼ teaspoon black pepper
½ teaspoon cumin
1¼ cup almond flour

Cook's Comment:

Poblano peppers are not normally very spicy, but their degree of heat can vary some. Remove the seeds and white membrane of peppers to help reduce the heat.

Directions:

Preheat broiler. Spray a 9 x 13-inch baking dish with cooking spray and set aside.

Arrange the poblano chiles on a baking sheet and broil 2–3 minutes per side until charred and black. Transfer hot charred chiles to a ziptop plastic bag and seal to close. Allow to steam for 10 minutes.

Preheat oven to 400° F.

Meanwhile, combine all salsa ingredients in a blender and purée to desired consistency. Transfer salsa to a medium sauce pan and bring to a boil over medium heat. Reduce heat and allow to simmer for 35–45 minutes or until thickened and reduced by half.

After 10 minutes, carefully remove the chiles from the bag and, using a knife, scrape the charred skins from the peppers. Cut a 3-inch slit down the side of the chiles and reach in to release seeds and membrane; discard. Repeat with remaining chiles, arranging the peppers in the prepared baking dish. Stuff each chile with 1 ounce of cheese.

In a medium bowl, whisk together the eggs, salt, pepper, cumin, and almond flour. Dip each chile into the egg-almond flour mixture, carefully rolling the pepper in the mixture, but not filling the pepper. Allow excess egg mixture to drip off the chile and return it to the baking dish; repeat with remaining chiles.

Bake chiles for 13–14 minutes. Serve hot with the warm salsa.

Yield: 4 servings, 2 chiles each

Nutrition Information (per serving):

561 calories; 39.8 g. fat; 308 mg. cholesterol; 735 mg. sodium; 26.0 g. carbohydrate; 12.3 g. fiber; 31.8 g. protein; 5.3 g. sugar

Spaghetti Squash with Mushroom Bolognese

Squash:

2 spaghetti squash, cut in half lengthwise

1 tablespoon extra-virgin olive oil

½ teaspoon salt

¼ teaspoon black pepper

½ cup almond flour

Bolognese:

2 teaspoons extra-virgin olive oil

½ onion, chopped

4 garlic cloves, minced

2 carrots, diced

2 celery stalks, diced

½ teaspoon salt

¼ teaspoon black pepper

12 oz. mushrooms, diced (cremini, shitake, oyster)

28 oz. low-sodium tomato sauce

14.5 oz. can whole tomatoes

2 tablespoons balsamic vinegar

1 teaspoon Italian seasoning

¼ teaspoon cinnamon

2 bay leaves

Nutrition Note:

Spaghetti squash is aptly named for its stringy insides, which can double as gluten-free, low-carb, vegan spaghetti.

Directions:

Preheat oven to 450° F.

Scoop the seeds out of each half of the squash and brush the flesh of the squash with olive oil; sprinkle with salt and pepper. Place squash halves, flesh side up, on baking sheets and roast for 30–40 minutes or until the "spaghetti" can easily be pulled out with a fork. In a large bowl, sprinkle the spaghetti squash strands with almond flour and toss well to coat and absorb any moisture. Cover with foil.

Meanwhile, to make the Bolognese, heat the olive oil in a large pot. Once hot, add the onion and sauté for 5 minutes or until softened. Add the garlic and stir constantly for 30 seconds or until fragrant.

Add the carrots, celery, salt, pepper, and mushrooms to the pot and cook an additional 5 minutes or until vegetables are slightly tender.

Add the remaining ingredients—tomato sauce through bay leaves—and stir. Bring to a simmer and simmer for 40–50 minutes.

Serve hot Bolognese over spaghetti squash

Yield: 6 servings

Nutrition Information (per serving):

225 calories; 8.5 g. fat; 0 mg. cholesterol; 499 mg. sodium; 29.7 g. carbohydrate; 9.2 g. fiber; 9.0 g. protein; 12.8 g. sugar

Wild Rice, Sausage, and Apple-Stuffed Acorn Squash

2 large acorn squash, halved and seeds removed

2 teaspoons extra-virgin olive oil, divided

½ cup dry wild rice

¼ onion, finely chopped

1 rib celery, finely chopped

¼ teaspoon salt

1 clove garlic, minced

8 oz. (2 links) spicy Italian turkey sausage, casings removed

1 tablespoon fresh sage, minced (or 1 teaspoon dried)

½ apple, finely diced

¼ cup unsweetened dried cranberries

¼ cup walnuts, chopped

¼ cup almond flour

Nutrition Note:

This recipe can easily be made vegetarian and vegan by omitting the sausage or made Paleo by omitting the rice. In either case, double up the onion, celery, and apple to ensure an adequate volume to stuff the acorn squash.

Directions:

Preheat oven to 400° F. Place the squash cut-side up on a baking sheet and brush with 1 teaspoon oil. Roast squash for 30–40 minutes or until just fork-tender. Remove from oven.

Meanwhile, combine the wild rice and ¾ cup water in a small pan and bring to a boil over medium-high heat. Stir the rice and cover with a lid; reduce heat to low and allow to simmer for 15 minutes. Remove pan from heat and allow to sit for 10–15 minutes.

In a small skillet, heat the remaining teaspoon of oil over medium heat. Once hot, add the onion, celery, and salt, and sauté for 2–3 minutes or until tender. Add the garlic and sauté an additional 30–60 seconds or until fragrant. Add the turkey sausage to the skillet and break up the meat with a wooden spoon. Heat until sausage is cooked through, about 5 minutes. Add the sage and apple to the pan and sauté an additional 2–3 minutes to warm through.

In a large bowl, combine the cooked wild rice, the sausage mixture, and the remaining ingredients: dried cranberries, walnuts, and almond flour; mix well. Stuff each squash half with the mixture, heaping the mixture if necessary. Bake the stuffed squash an additional 15 minutes. Allow to cool for 2–3 minutes.

Yield: 4 servings (1 stuffed squash half each)

Nutrition Information (per serving):

385 calories; 15.8 g. fat; 30 mg. cholesterol; 495 mg. sodium; 52.5 g. carbohydrate; 7.3 g. fiber; 14.8 g. protein; 8.0 g. sugar

Not Quite Vodka Sauce

4 lbs tomatoes, quartered
¼ cup extra-virgin olive oil
1 teaspoon salt
6 cloves garlic, peeled

⅓ cup almond flour
⅓ cup half-and-half
½ cup fresh basil, chopped

Directions:

Preheat oven to 450° F.

In a 9 x 13-inch baking dish, toss the tomatoes with the olive oil and sprinkle with salt. Roast the tomatoes for 25 minutes.

Transfer tomatoes and accumulated juices to a large pot, place over medium-high heat, and bring to a boil. Once boiling, reduce heat to medium-low and stir in almond flour. Allow sauce to simmer 40–50 minutes or until reduced by about one-third.

Using an immersion blender, purée the tomatoes to desired consistency. Stir in the half-and-half and remove from heat. Stir in basil and serve immediately.

Yield: ~5¼ cups (7 servings; ¾ cup each)

Nutrition Information (per serving):

169 calories; 12.6 g. fat; 6 mg. cholesterol; 339 mg. sodium; 12.9 g. carbohydrate; 3.9 g. fiber; 4.3 g. protein; 7.6 g. sugar

Fun Fact:

Traditional vodka sauces use the alcohol to bring out the flavors of the tomatoes. Use in-season, perfectly ripe tomatoes, however, and there's no need for the vodka! Plus, this recipe uses half-and-half versus the traditional heavy cream to keep the calories down.

Caprese Quinoa Bake with Balsamic Reduction

1 cup dry quinoa

2 cups water

¾ teaspoon salt

½ teaspoon black pepper

¼ cup + 3 tablespoons fresh basil,
chopped and divided

3 large tomatoes or 6 small

tomatoes, sliced into ¼-inch thick slices

6 oz. fresh mozzarella

½ cup balsamic vinegar

¼ cup almond flour

1 oz. Parmigiano-Reggiano, grated

Cook's Comment:

In place of using an egg, almond flour acts as the "binder" to keep this bake easy to sere in single pieces.

Directions:

Rinse quinoa under cold running water in a fine mesh strainer for 1–2 minutes. Drain and transfer to a small pan, along with 2 cups of water. Place pot over medium-high heat and bring to a boil. Stir, cover, and reduce heat to low. Simmer quinoa for 15 minutes, remove from heat, and allow to sit for 10–15 minutes.

Preheat oven to 375° F.

In a medium bowl, combine the cooked quinoa, salt, pepper, and ¼ cup basil; stir.

Spray an 8 x 8-inch baking dish with nonstick cooking spray and layer the bottom with half the tomato slices. Top the tomatoes with the quinoa and press the quinoa gently into an even layer using the back of a spatula, reaching the sides and corners of the pan. Tear the mozzarella into small pieces and place over the quinoa. Layer the remaining tomatoes on top of the mozzarella and bake for 15 minutes.

In a small sauce pan, heat the balsamic vinegar over medium-low heat. Simmer for 10–15 minutes or until reduced by half and consistency is syrupy. Stir often to avoid burning.

In a small dish, combine the almond flour and Parmigiano-Reggiano; mix well. After 15 minutes of baking, remove quinoa bake from the oven and sprinkle with almond flour mixture. Change oven setting to broil and return bake to the oven. Broil for 30–90 seconds, being sure to avoid burning. Remove from oven. Drizzle with balsamic reduction and sprinkle with reserved 3 tablespoons basil.

Yield: 4 servings

Nutrition Information (per serving):

390 calories; 16.0 g. fat; 36 mg. cholesterol; 555 mg. sodium; 42.0 g. carbohydrate; 5.8 g. fiber; 20.0 g. protein; 10.8 g. sugar

Baked Cod with Dill Aioli

Aioli:
2 tablespoons light mayonnaise
2 tablespoons nonfat plain
   Greek yogurt
1 garlic clove, minced
1 tablespoon fresh dill, minced
¼ teaspoon ground black
   pepper
1 teaspoon extra-virgin olive oil

Fish:
3 (5 oz.) cod filets
½ cup almond flour
¼ teaspoon garlic powder
1 tablespoon grated Parmesan
   cheese
1 tablespoon flat-leaf parsley,
   minced
⅛ teaspoon salt
⅛ teaspoon ground black
   pepper
Olive oil mister

Nutrition Note:

Almond flour may not only be the tastiest breading for seafood and poultry, but also the healthiest.

Directions:

Preheat oven to 425° F. Line a baking sheet with parchment and set aside.

In a small dish, combine all of the aioli ingredients and mix well; set aside.

Blot the cod on paper towels to absorb excess moisture.

Combine the almond flour, garlic powder, Parmesan, parsley, salt, and pepper in a shallow dish; mix to combine well. Dredge each cod filet in the almond flour mixture, coating both sides of the fish. Repeat with remaining filets and transfer cod to the baking sheet. Mist the filets with olive oil.

Bake fish 12–14 minutes or until slightly browned and fish is flaky. Serve hot with aioli to accompany.

Yield: 3 servings with 1½ tablespoons aioli each

Nutrition Information (per serving):

272 calories; 14.3 g. fat; 55 mg. cholesterol; 334 mg. sodium; 5.3 g. carbohydrate; 2.0 g. fiber; 30.7 g. protein; 1.0 g. sugar

Shrimp, Pesto, and Goat Cheese Pizza

Crust:

1 cup warm water (110–115° F)

1 teaspoon brown sugar

1½ teaspoons rapid-rise active
    dry yeast

½ cup tapioca starch

½ cup sorghum flour

½ cup potato starch

½ cup blanched almond flour

½ cup millet flour

1 tablespoon coconut flour

1½ teaspoon baking powder

1 teaspoon Xanthan gum

½ teaspoon salt

Topping:

2 cups (2 oz.) fresh basil, firmly
    packed

¼ cup pine nuts

2 cloves garlic

¼ teaspoon salt

¼ cup + 1 teaspoon extra-virgin
    olive oil, divided

1 lb small raw shrimp, peeled
    and deveined

⅛ teaspoon salt and black
    pepper, to taste

5 oz. goat cheese

2 tablespoons (½ oz.)
    Parmigiano-Reggiano,
    grated

Cook's Comment:

It's a fact—making gluten-free pizza crust is no easy task. It can't be accomplished with just one gluten-free flour, but rather requires a variety of flours that all contribute to making a sturdy, slightly crispy crust that isn't dry, doughy, or completely limp. I hope you love this pizza crust as much as I do!

Directions:

To make the pesto, combine the basil, pine nuts, garlic, ¼ teaspoon salt, and ¼ cup olive oil in the bowl of a mini food processor, food prep, or blender. Blend well, pulsing for 10 seconds at a time until a smooth consistency is achieved; set aside.

In a small skillet over medium-high heat, heat the remaining teaspoon of olive oil. Add the shrimp to the pan and season with ⅛ teaspoon salt and black pepper to taste. Sauté shrimp 2–3 minutes or until they are just pink; remove shrimp to a plate lined with paper towels.

Preheat oven to 400° F.

In a small bowl, combine the warm water, brown sugar, and yeast; allow to sit for 5 minutes.

Meanwhile, whisk together the tapioca starch, sorghum flour, potato starch, almond flour, millet flour, coconut flour, baking powder, Xanthan gum, and salt. Add the water and mix with a wooden spoon. Knead the dough to form a smooth ball.

Roll the dough between 2 sheets of parchment paper until it is approximately 16 inches in diameter; transfer to a pizza pan.

Par-bake the crust for 5–7 minutes and remove from oven. Spread the pesto over the surface of the crust, top with goat cheese, shrimp, and Parmigiano-Reggiano. Bake pizza for an additional 8–10 minutes.

Yield: 8 large slices

Nutrition Information (per slice):

366 calories; 18.1 g. fat; 83 mg. cholesterol; 522 mg. sodium; 33.3 g. carbohydrate; 3.6 g. fiber; 18.8 g. protein; 1.0 g. sugar

Quick Breads, Muffins, and More

Blueberry Coconut Muffins

2 cups blanched almond flour
½ cup coconut flour
1½ teaspoon baking soda
1 teaspoon salt
6 eggs
1 cup unsweetened applesauce
1 teaspoon vanilla extract
½ cup honey
1¼ cup fresh or frozen
  blueberries
⅓ cup unsweetened coconut
  flakes

Directions:

Preheat oven to 350° F. Mist a muffin tin with nonstick cooking spray and set aside.

In a large bowl, whisk together the almond flour, coconut flour, baking soda, and salt.

In a separate medium bowl, whisk to combine the eggs, applesauce, vanilla, and honey.

Mix the wet ingredients into the dry, mixing until combined. Fold in the blueberries and coconut. Fill each muffin well two-thirds full and bake for 25–27 minutes or until an inserted toothpick comes out cleanly. Allow muffins to cool completely.

Store muffins in an air-tight container in the refrigerator up to four days.

Yield: 18 muffins

Nutrition Information (per muffin):

157 calories; 9.1 g. fat; 62 mg. cholesterol; 261 mg. sodium; 15.4 g. carbohydrate; 3.9 g. fiber; 5.5 g. protein; 8.9 g. sugar

Cook's Comment:

These muffins freeze really well. Coconut lovers, you'll go crazy for these. The coconut flakes make these muffins something special. It's hard to believe they're less than 160 calories each.

Almond-Oat Bread

1½ cups blanched almond flour

½ cup gluten-free oat flour

1 tablespoon coconut flour

½ teaspoon salt

¾ teaspoon baking soda

5 eggs

1½ tablespoons olive oil

1 tablespoon honey

1 teaspoon gluten-free oats

Cooking spray

Directions:

Preheat oven to 350° F.

In a large bowl, whisk to combine the almond flour, oat flour, coconut flour, salt, and baking soda; set aside.

In a medium bowl, gently whisk the eggs. Add the oil and honey, whisking well to combine.

Add the wet ingredients to the dry and stir to mix well. Transfer the batter to a standard loaf pan that has been sprayed with cooking spray. Sprinkle batter with oats. Bake for 30 minutes or until golden and an inserted toothpick comes out cleanly from the center of the loaf.

Allow bread to cool completely before slicing. Store in the refrigerator.

Yield: 12 slices

Nutrition Information (per slice):

148 calories; 11.3 g. fat; 77 mg. cholesterol; 206 mg. sodium; 7.6 g. carbohydrate; 2.3 g. fiber; 5.7 g. protein; 2.0 g. sugar

Fun Fact:

This is one of my favorite recipes throughout my gluten-free experimentation. This bread is absolutely wonderful and comes in at 7.6 grams of carbohydrate, under 150 calories per slice, and tastes good. Yes, you have to taste it to believe it!

Herbed Buttermilk Drop Biscuits

1¼ cup blanched almond flour
½ cup garbanzo bean flour
1 tablespoon fresh herbs, minced (thyme, oregano, etc.)
1 teaspoon baking powder
½ teaspoon salt
1 teaspoon granulated sugar
2 tablespoons unsalted butter
½ cup low-fat buttermilk

Directions:

Preheat oven to 425° F. Line a baking sheet with parchment paper and set aside.

In a medium bowl, combine the almond flour, garbanzo bean flour, herbs, baking powder, salt, and sugar; whisk well.

In a microwave-safe dish, melt the butter on high for 45–60 seconds or until bubbling hot and melted. Slowly whisk the butter into the buttermilk.

Add the buttermilk mixture to the dry ingredients, and mix well.

Drop the biscuit batter by heaping ¼-cup scoopfuls onto the lined baking sheet. Bake biscuits for 10 minutes or until slightly browned. Allow to cool before serving.

Yield: 8 biscuits

Nutrition Information (per biscuit):

162 calories; 12.1 g. fat; 8 mg. cholesterol; 221 mg. sodium; 9.8 g. carbohydrate; 3.3 g. fiber; 5.8 g. protein; 2.6 g. sugar

Cook's Comment:

Garbanzo bean flour has a very strong, bean-y flavor. It is best suited for savory recipes and used in lesser proportions than other flours. Striking the perfect ratio of garbanzo bean flour to other gluten-free flours can yield great results, as is the case in these biscuits.

Cranberry, Pumpkin, and Walnut Loaf

2 cups blanched almond flour

¾ teaspoon baking soda

½ teaspoon salt

½ teaspoon ground nutmeg

¾ teaspoon cinnamon

Pinch of ground ginger

2 large eggs

¼ cup unsweetened applesauce

¼ cup honey

½ cup pumpkin purée

⅓ cup walnuts

¾ cup fresh or frozen whole cranberries

Directions:

Preheat oven to 350° F. Lightly mist a standard loaf pan with cooking spray; set aside.

In a large bowl, whisk to combine the almond flour, baking soda, salt, nutmeg, cinnamon, and ginger. Set aside.

In a medium bowl, lightly beat the eggs with a whisk or fork. Add the applesauce, honey, and pumpkin purée, whisking well to combine.

Add the wet ingredients into the dry and mix to combine until the mixture is cohesive. Fold in the walnuts and cranberries; distribute well.

Transfer the mixture into the loaf pan and spread evenly, reaching the corners of the pan.

Bake for 45–50 minutes or until an inserted toothpick comes out clean. Allow to cool for at least 20–30 minutes on a wire rack before slicing or removing the bread from the loaf pan.

Yield: 10 slices

Nutrition Information (per slice):

201 calories; 14.4 g. fat; 37.0 mg. cholesterol; 229 mg. sodium; 14.8 g. carbohydrate; 3.6 g. fiber; 6.7 g. protein; 8.5 g. sugar

Nutrition Note:

Most recipes using unsweetened cranberries are high in sugar. By using honey, which is naturally very sweet, and unsweetened applesauce as a natural, lower-calorie sweetener option, the sugar and carbohydrate content in this recipe are kept down.

Cherry-Oat Muffins

2 cups blanched almond flour

1 cup gluten-free old-fashioned oats

¾ teaspoon baking soda

½ teaspoon baking powder

¼ teaspoon salt

¼ cup sucanat or other granular sugar

2 eggs

¼ cup coconut oil, melted and cooled

1 teaspoon vanilla extract

¼ cup unsweetened applesauce

1 cup cherries, pitted and quartered

Directions:

Preheat oven to 350° F. Line a standard muffin tin with 12 muffin liners and set aside.

In a large bowl, combine the almond flour, oats, baking soda, baking powder, salt, and sucanat. Whisk well to thoroughly combine and set aside.

In a medium bowl, lightly beat the eggs. Add the coconut oil, vanilla extract, and applesauce; whisk well to combine.

Stir the wet ingredients into the dry until well-combined and cohesive. Gently fold in the cherries.

Drop the batter into the muffin wells by the ¼ cup. Bake for 20–22 minutes or until an inserted toothpick comes out clean. Allow to cool completely before serving.

Yield: 12 muffins

Nutrition Information (per muffin):

208 calories; 15.3 g. fat; 31 mg. cholesterol; 162 mg. sodium; 15.0 g. carbohydrate; 2.9 g. fiber; 5.9 g. protein; 2.2 g. sugar

Cook's Comment:

The combination of almond flour, oat flour, and coconut oil makes for a perfect crumb in a muffin. These taste incredibly rich thanks to the various, flavorful fat sources in the recipe—eggs, almond flour, and coconut oil.

Almond and Corn Tortillas

3 cups masa harina
1 cup almond flour
½ teaspoon salt

2 cups warm water, plus more if
    needed

Directions:

Line a tortilla press with pieces of plastic wrap or parchment on both the top and bottom plates.

In a large bowl, whisk together the masa harina, almond flour, and salt. Pour in the water and mix well until a Play-Doh consistency forms.

Heat one (or two) small, nonstick skillet(s) over medium-high heat.

Working one at a time, pinch off a 1½-inch round piece of dough and roll into a ball. Cover remaining dough with a damp towel to keep moist while working.

Arrange the piece of dough on the bottom of the tortilla press and on top of the plastic or parchment; top with an additional piece of plastic or parchment before closing the tortilla press to create a 6- to 7-inch tortilla. Carefully peel the tortilla off the plastic or parchment and transfer to the hot skillet.

Cook tortillas 2–3 minutes before flipping and cooking an additional 1–2 minutes. Tortillas may be fragile; flip carefully.

Once cooked, transfer tortillas to a tortilla warmer or a plate layered with a moist paper towel and covered with tin foil or another covering to trap in heat and moisture.

Repeat with remaining dough.

Yield: 20 tortillas

Nutrition Information (per tortilla):

92 calories; 3.4 g. fat; 0 mg. cholesterol; 60 mg. sodium; 13.8 g. carbohydrate; 1.8 g. fiber; 3.0 g. protein; 0.2 g. sugar

Cook's Comment:

There are three key components to making the perfect tortilla. First, practice—you won't get it right the first time, and that's okay. Second, a tortilla press—you need one. I'll save you the frustration of finding out the hard way. Last, you need moisture—keep the dough moist, as well as the cooked tortillas. It's a must.

Classic Banana Bread

1½ cups blanched almond flour
½ cup coconut flour
1½ teaspoons baking soda
1 teaspoon salt

4 over-ripe bananas, mashed
6 large eggs
1 teaspoon pure vanilla extract
½ cup raw honey

Directions:

Preheat oven to 350° F. Mist four mini loaf tins with nonstick cooking spray and set aside.

In a large bowl, whisk to combine the almond flour, coconut flour, baking soda, and salt; set aside.

In a medium bowl, mash the bananas against the sides of the bowl using the back of a fork. To the bananas, add the eggs, vanilla, and honey; whisk well to combine.

Add the wet ingredients into the dry and mix. Distribute the batter between each of the four mini loaf tins and bake for 30 minutes, or until an inserted toothpick is cleanly removed.

Allow to cool completely before slicing.

Yield: 4 mini loaves with 4 servings each (16 slices/servings)

Nutrition Information (per ¼ mini loaf):

160 calories; 7.6 g. fat; 69 mg. cholesterol; 291 mg. sodium; 19.9 g. carbohydrate; 3.9 g. fiber; 5.7 g. protein; 12.9 g. sugar

Nutrition Note:

For those looking to increase omega-3 fatty acids in the diet, add walnuts to this recipe—simply fold them into the batter before distributing the batter between the loaf tins. Not only are walnuts traditional and tasty in banana bread, but their nutritional perks are endless.

Rosemary and Cracked Pepper Dinner Rolls

1 cup sorghum flour

1 cup tapioca starch

¼ cup garbanzo bean flour

½ cup millet flour

½ cup almond flour

¼ cup coconut flour

1 teaspoon Xanthan gum

1 teaspoon salt

1½ teaspoon freshly cracked black pepper

1½ teaspoon sugar

2¼ teaspoons (1 packet) rapid-rise yeast

1½ cups low-fat buttermilk

2 eggs

¼ cup extra-virgin olive oil

1 tablespoon fresh rosemary, minced

Shopping Tip:

Xanthan gum is generally found near the baking goods and pantry staples. It is pricey, but because you use so little at a time, it lasts forever.

Directions:

In the bowl of a stand mixer fitted with the dough hook attachment, combine the sorghum flour, tapioca starch, garbanzo bean flour, millet flour, almond flour, coconut flour, Xanthan gum, salt, pepper, sugar, and yeast. On medium speed, allow hook to mix ingredients for 1–2 minutes.

Heat the buttermilk in a microwave-safe container for 45–60 seconds on high heat (should be warm to the touch, but not hot). Add the warm buttermilk, eggs, oil, and rosemary to the stand mixer bowl and continue mixing the bread for 2–3 minutes or until ingredients are incorporated into a dough.

Cover the stand mixer bowl with a warm, damp rag and place in a warm location to rise for 45 minutes. The dough will not rise significantly, but it will become airy and less dense.

Roll the dough into 2-inch, round balls and place in a greased baking dish, spaced 1 inch apart. Bake the rolls for 20–22 minutes or until they begin to turn golden. Best served warm.

Yield: 12 rolls

Nutrition Information (per roll):

205 calories; 8.8 g. fat; 32 mg. cholesterol; 228 mg. sodium; 26.6 g. carbohydrate; 3.9 g. fiber; 5.9 g. protein; 2.7 g. sugar

Lemon Poppyseed Muffins

1 cup sorghum flour
1¼ cup blanched almond flour
½ cup tapioca starch
2 teaspoons baking powder
½ teaspoon baking soda
½ teaspoon salt

3 eggs
¼ cup freshly squeezed lemon
  juice
¾ cup honey
1½ tablespoon poppyseeds

Directions:

Preheat oven to 350° F. Line a muffin tin with 12 liners and set aside.

In a large bowl, whisk together the sorghum flour, almond flour, tapioca starch, baking powder, baking soda, and salt.

In a medium bowl, whisk to combine the eggs, lemon juice, and honey. Mix in the poppyseeds and pour the wet ingredients into the dry. With a rubber spatula, mix well.

Fill muffin wells with approximately 1/3 cup batter and bake for 16–18 minutes, or until slightly browned. Allow to cool. Best served warm.

Yield: 12 muffins

Nutrition Information (per muffin):

211 calories; 7.4 g. fat; 46 mg. cholesterol; 249 mg. sodium; 32.9 g. carbohydrate; 2.3 g. fiber; 5.4 g. protein; 17.8 g. sugar

Nutrition Note:

Recipes with large amounts of citrus juice, such as lemon, require a bit more sweetener. The generous use of honey in this recipe sends the carbohydrate and sugar content up some, but the result is still sinless and delicious.

Jalapeño Cheddar Cornbread

1 cup almond flour
¾ cup cornmeal
1 teaspoon baking powder
¼ teaspoon salt
2 tablespoons sugar
2 eggs

¼ cup olive oil
½ cup nonfat milk
2 jalapeños, seeded and minced
½ cup (2 oz.) 2% cheddar
   cheese, shredded

Nutrition Note:

Low-carb cornbread made without butter? Neat, right? The almond flour allows for a rich piece of cornbread with none of the guilt.

Directions:

Preheat oven to 375° F. Mist a 9-inch baking pan with nonstick cooking spray and set aside.

In a medium bowl, whisk together the almond flour, cornmeal, baking powder, salt, and sugar.

In a separate medium bowl, whisk to combine the eggs, oil, and milk.

Mix the wet ingredients into the dry until mixed well and no dry spots remain. Fold in the jalapeños and cheese.

Transfer batter to the pan and bake for 24–26 minutes or just beginning to brown around the edges.

Yield: 16 squares

Nutrition Information (per square):

120 calories; 8.5 g. fat; 26 mg. cholesterol; 110 mg. sodium; 8.8 g. carbohydrate; 1.3 g. fiber; 3.9 g. protein; 2.2 g. sugar

Peanut Butter–Banana Muffins

2 cups blanched almond flour

¾ teaspoon baking soda

½ teaspoon baking powder

¼ teaspoon salt

2 over-ripe bananas, peeled (8 oz.)

2 eggs

¼ cup natural peanut butter

2 tablespoons pure maple syrup

1 tablespoon olive oil

¼ cup (about 10) unsalted walnut halves

Directions:

Preheat oven to 350° F. Line a standard muffin tin with 10 muffin liners and set aside.

In a large bowl, combine the almond flour, baking soda, baking powder, and salt. Whisk well to thoroughly combine and set aside.

In a medium bowl, mash the bananas with the back of a fork against the side of the bowl. Add the eggs and whisk well. Add the peanut butter, maple syrup, and olive oil; whisk well.

Stir the wet ingredients into the dry until well-combined and cohesive.

Drop the batter into the muffin wells by the ¼ cup and top each with a walnut half. Bake for 25–28 minutes or until an inserted toothpick comes out clean. Allow to cool completely before serving.

Yield: 10 muffins

Nutrition Information (per muffin):

240 calories; 18.5 g. fat; 37.0 mg. cholesterol; 225 mg. sodium; 14.6 g. carbohydrate; 5.7 g. fiber; 8.3 g. protein; 6.5 g. sugar

Cook's Comment:

Subtly sweet thanks to bananas and just a bit of maple syrup, these muffins have a phenomenal consistency. For those who are looking for a traditional muffin texture, try these!

Feta and Sun-Dried Tomato Mini Loaves

1 cup blanched almond flour
¾ cup potato starch
½ cup millet flour
¼ cup garbanzo bean flour
½ teaspoon salt
¾ teaspoon baking soda

5 eggs
¼ cup olive oil
6 sun-dried tomatoes,
    olive oil-packed, diced
1½ oz. (about ⅓ cup) feta,
    crumbled

Directions:

Preheat oven to 350° F. Mist four mini loaf pans with nonstick cooking spray; set aside.

In a medium bowl, whisk together the almond flour, potato starch, millet flour, garbanzo bean flour, salt, and baking soda; set aside.

In a medium bowl, whisk the eggs. Add the oil and whisk well to combine.

Pour the wet ingredients into the dry and mix with a rubber spatula. Fold the sun-dried tomatoes and feta into the mixture.

Distribute the batter between four mini loaf pans, smoothing out the tops with the back of the rubber spatula. Bake for 24–25 minutes or until just beginning to turn golden. Allow to cool 10 minutes before removing from the loaf pans and slicing. Store loaves in an air-tight container in the refrigerator.

Yield: 4 mini loaves (16 servings; about 4 servings per loaf)

Nutrition Information (per ¼ loaf):

153 calories; 9.4 g. fat; 58 mg. cholesterol; 146 mg. sodium; 13.6 g. carbohydrate; 1.6 g. fiber; 4.8 g. protein; 0.8 g. sugar

Cook's Comment:

Baking in mini loaf pans helps from exposing to heat for long periods of time, which can create dry, crumbly bread.

Herbed Honey Muffins

1 cup almond flour

1 cup sorghum flour

½ cup tapioca starch

2 teaspoons baking powder

½ teaspoon baking soda

½ teaspoon salt

3 eggs

½ cup honey

1 tablespoon fresh rosemary, minced

Directions:

Preheat oven to 350° F. Line a cupcake tin with 12 muffin liners and set aside.

In a medium bowl, whisk to combine the almond flour, sorghum flour, tapioca starch, baking powder, baking soda, and salt.

In a separate medium bowl, lightly beat the eggs. Whisk in the honey, mixing well.

Pour the honey mixture into the dry ingredients and mix with a rubber spatula. Fold in the rosemary.

Fill each muffin well with ¼ to 1/3 cup of the batter. Bake muffins for 17–18 minutes or until an inserted toothpick is cleanly removed.

Yield: 12 muffins

Nutrition Information (per muffin):

170 calories; 6.3 g. fat; 46 mg. cholesterol; 248 mg. sodium; 26.2 g. carbohydrate; 2.0 g. fiber; 4.8 g. protein; 11.8 g. sugar

Cook's Comment:

Honey and rosemary are one of my favorite flavor combinations—it's so earthy and fragrant. These muffins are unique and perfect as a snack on their own or as an accompaniment to any meal—breakfast, lunch, or dinner.

Desserts

Coconut Thumbprints

1½ cups blanched almond flour
½ cup potato starch
½ cup sorghum flour
¼ cup tapioca starch
2 tablespoons coconut flour
½ teaspoon baking soda
½ teaspoon salt
⅓ cup coconut oil (solid)
¼ cup sucanat or other granular sugar
2 eggs
¼ cup honey
1 tablespoon vanilla extract
¾ cup unsweetened coconut flakes
5 tablespoons reduced sugar jam

Shopping Tip:

While most jams are gluten-free, be sure to double-check labels, especially when purchasing anything out of a package, box, jar, or can.

Directions:

In a large bowl, whisk together the almond flour, potato starch, sorghum flour, tapioca starch, coconut flour, baking soda, and salt.

In the bowl of a stand mixer fitted with the paddle attachment or in a large bowl with an electric hand mixer, cream together the coconut oil and sugar until light and fluffy, about 2 minutes. Add the eggs one at a time, mixing well between additions. Add the honey and vanilla; mix well.

In several additions, add the flour mixture to the wet ingredients, mixing well between each addition. The dough should be moist, but workable.

Roll the dough into 1¼-inch rounds and roll in the coconut flakes. Transfer dough to baking sheets, 2 inches apart. Press the pad of your thumb into the tops of each cookie to create a small well. Fill the well with ½ teaspoon jam. Repeat with remaining dough and jam.

Bake cookies for 10–12 minutes or until golden. Allow to cool for 5 minutes on the cookie sheets before transferring to wire cooling racks to cool completely.

Yield: 30 cookies

Nutrition Information (per cookie):

115 calories; 6.9 g. fat; 12 mg. cholesterol; 65 mg. sodium; 12.5 g. carbohydrate; 1.4 g. fiber; 2.0 g. protein; 4.0 g. sugar

Bing Cherry Crumble

1½ lbs bing cherries, pitted and halved

Squeeze of lemon juice

1 tablespoon tapioca starch

¼ cup + 1 tablespoon sucanat, divided

½ cup almond flour

½ cup gluten-free old-fashioned oats

¼ teaspoon cinnamon

⅛ teaspoon salt

3 tablespoons coconut oil, solid

Directions:

Preheat oven to 350° F.

In a 2-quart casserole dish, combine the cherries, lemon juice, tapioca starch, and 1 tablespoon of the sucanat. Toss well and allow the cherries to absorb the starch.

In the bowl of a food processor, combine the remaining ¼ cup sucanat, almond flour, oats, cinnamon, salt, and coconut oil. Pulse the mixture 10–20 times or until the mixture is mealy and clumps. Using your fingers, gently break up the crumble mixture over the top of the cherries, spreading the mixture over the entire surface.

Bake crumble for 35–40 minutes or until bubbly and lightly browned on top. Serve warm or at room temperature.

Yield: 5 servings (scant 1 cup each)

Nutrition Information (per serving):

259 calories; 12.8 g. fat; 18 mg. cholesterol; 64 mg. sodium; 35.8 g. carbohydrate; 3.2 g. fiber; 4.0 g. protein; 10.2 g. sugar

Cook's Comment:

Frozen cherries will work just fine in this recipe; however, fresh are even better. Invest $10 in a cherry pitter that will make prepping the cherries go much faster.

Light and Fluffy Chocolate Cake

1½ cups blanched almond flour

⅓ cup unsweetened cocoa powder

½ teaspoon baking soda

½ teaspoon salt

3 eggs

½ cup honey

½ cup coconut oil, melted and cooled

1 tablespoon vanilla extract

1 teaspoon instant espresso powder (optional)

¼ cup dark chocolate chips

Directions:

Preheat oven to 350° F. Mist an 8 x 8-inch baking dish with cooking oil; set aside.

In a large bowl, whisk to combine the almond flour, cocoa, baking soda, and salt.

In a medium bowl, whisk the eggs. Add the honey, melted and cooled coconut oil, vanilla, and espresso powder.

Mix the wet ingredients into the dry, combining well. Fold in the chocolate chips. Transfer batter to the baking dish and spread to the corners evenly.

Bake cake for 25–30 minutes or until top is shiny and brownies are set. Allow to cool before slicing and serving.

Yield: 16 2-inch square pieces of cake

Nutrition Information (per piece):

189 calories; 14.5 g. fat; 35 mg. cholesterol; 128 mg. sodium;
14.1 g. carbohydrate; 1.7 g. fiber; 3.9 g. protein; 10.8 g. sugar

Nutrition Note:

The eggs and baking soda create a leavened cake that is fluffy and light. Its texture, not its taste, match these impressive nutrition stats.

Shopping Tip:

When purchasing dark chocolate, check the ingredient list to be sure the product is, in fact, dairy-free. Often, milk or milk constituents are added in the manufacturing process.

Oatmeal Raisin Cookies

1½ cups blanched almond flour
1¼ cup gluten-free oats
1 teaspoon baking soda
½ teaspoon salt
½ teaspoon ground cinnamon
2 eggs
½ cup brown sugar
¼ cup olive oil
¼ cup unsweetened apple-
    sauce
1 tablespoon vanilla extract
½ cup raisins

Directions:

Preheat oven to 350° F.

In a large bowl, mix together the almond flour, oats, baking soda, salt, and cinnamon.

In a separate medium bowl, lightly beat the eggs. Add the brown sugar, oil, applesauce, and vanilla; mix well with a wire whisk.

Add the dry ingredients to the wet and mix well; fold in raisins.

Drop the cookies in 2 tablespoon heaps and flatten slightly using the palm of your hand. Bake cookies for 15–16 minutes or until slightly golden.

Yield: 18 cookies

Nutrition Information (per cookie):

145 calories; 8.7 g. fat; 21 mg. cholesterol; 143 mg. sodium; 15.0 g. carbohydrate; 1.9 g. fiber; 3.5 g. protein; 9.1 g. sugar

Fun Fact:

You'd never know these cookies were gluten-free—they're that close to "the real deal"!

Chocolate Chip Cupcakes with Chocolate–Peanut Butter Frosting

Cupcakes:
2½ cups almond flour
½ cup tapioca starch
2 teaspoons baking powder
½ teaspoon baking soda
½ teaspoon salt
3 eggs
$^{1}/_{3}$ cup honey
$^{1}/_{3}$ cup olive oil
1 teaspoon vanilla extract
$^{1}/_{3}$ cup mini dark chocolate
    chips

Frosting:
¾ cup creamy natural peanut
    butter
¼ cup unsweetened cocoa
    powder
½ cup powdered sugar
¼ cup + 2 tablespoons un-
    sweetened vanilla almond
    milk

Fun Fact:

Creating a cupcake recipe that was actually good was really difficult to achieve. They would always end up too dry and dense, or so moist and heavy they wouldn't leaven. These, however, are the labor of love and commitment to the perfect gluten-free cupcake. They're even good without the frosting for a lower-calorie dessert!

Directions:

Preheat oven to 350° F. Line a muffin tin with 12 liners.

In a medium bowl, whisk together the almond flour, tapioca starch, baking powder, baking soda, and salt. Set aside.

In a medium bowl, whisk together the eggs, honey, olive oil, and vanilla extract.

Add the wet ingredients to the dry and mix well; fold in chocolate chips. Drop batter by rounded scoopfuls into wells of the muffin tin.

Bake for 15–18 minutes or until an inserted toothpick comes out cleanly and cupcake tops turn golden; allow cupcakes to cool completely.

While cupcakes cool, mix together the frosting ingredients in the bowl of a stand mixer or in a medium bowl with a hand mixer. Mix well and frost cupcakes as desired.

Yield: 12 frosted cupcakes

Nutrition Information (per cupcake):

402 calories; 28.8 g. fat; 46 mg. cholesterol; 332 mg. sodium; 30.4 g. carbohydrate; 3.8 g. fiber; 10.8 g. protein; 14.8 g. sugar

Apple Pie Shooters

Crumble:

1 cup almond flour

½ cup gluten-free oats

¼ teaspoon salt

¼ cup brown sugar

¼ teaspoon cinnamon

3 tablespoons coconut oil, solid

Apples:

4 apples, peeled, cored, and diced

¼ teaspoon cinnamon

3 tablespoons brown sugar

Nutrition Note:

Offering desserts in pre-portioned servings can help keep people on track with weight loss and managing their nutritional goals. Plus, they make for a creative and fun presentation!

Directions:

Preheat oven to 350° F.

In the bowl of a food processor, combine the almond flour, oats, salt, brown sugar, and cinnamon; pulse to combine. Drop the coconut oil into the food processor in small pieces, pulsing to create a crumbly mixture. Spread the mixture onto a baking sheet and bake for 15–16 minutes stirring halfway through baking. Note: Watch the crumble during the last few minutes of baking to ensure it does not burn.

Meanwhile, combine apples, cinnamon, and brown sugar in a medium pan and heat over medium heat, stirring often. Cook apples until softened and caramelized with the sugar, about 8–12 minutes.

To assemble, layer about 1 tablespoon of crumble with 2 tablespoons apples, repeated twice, and finish off with a teaspoon of crumble. Repeat layered apple pie in each shooter and serve warm or at room temperature.

Yield: 12 shooters (3 ounces each)

Nutrition Information (per shooter):

142 calories; 7.8 g. fat; 8 mg. cholesterol; 51 mg. sodium; 16.7 g. carbohydrate; 2.1 g. fiber; 2.5 g. protein; 12.1 g. sugar

Fudgy Mint Brownies

1¼ cup blanched almond flour
¼ cup unsweetened cocoa
    powder
¼ teaspoon salt
2 eggs
½ cup coconut oil, melted and
    cooled

½ cup honey
1 teaspoon instant espresso
    powder
½ teaspoon mint extract
½ cup dark chocolate chips

Directions:

Preheat oven to 350° F. Mist an 8 x 8-inch baking pan with nonstick spray and set aside.

In a medium bowl, whisk together the almond flour, cocoa powder, and salt.

In a separate medium bowl, gently beat the eggs to break them up. While whisking constantly, add the coconut oil and honey. Whisk well to combine. Add the espresso powder and mint extract; mix well.

Add the wet ingredients to the dry and mix well with a rubber spatula; fold in the chocolate chips. Transfer batter to the baking dish and bake for 30 minutes. Allow to cool to room temperature, then transfer to the refrigerator for at least 1 hour before cutting servings. Brownies are best stored and served chilled.

Yield: 16 brownies

Nutrition Information (per brownie):

191 calories; 14.1 g. fat; 23 mg. cholesterol; 48 mg. sodium; 15.8 g. carbohydrate; 1.2 g. fiber; 2.9 g. protein; 8.9 g. sugar

Cook's Comment:

These brownies are very dense and rich. They rightfully earn their name as "fudgy"—yum!

Golden Raisin Cookies

2½ cups blanched almond flour
½ teaspoon ground cinnamon
½ teaspoon salt
1 egg
¼ cup olive oil

⅓ cup pumpkin purée
¼ cup pure maple syrup
1 teaspoon vanilla extract
½ cup golden raisins

Directions:

Preheat oven to 350° F. Line two baking sheets with parchment paper and set aside.

In a medium bowl, whisk to combine the almond flour, cinnamon, and salt; set aside.

In a separate medium bowl, whisk the egg. To the egg, add the olive oil, pumpkin purée, maple syrup, and vanilla; whisk well.

Pour the wet ingredients into the dry and mix well; fold in the raisins.

Drop cookies by 2 tablespoon scoops onto the parchment paper and gently flatten slightly with fingers. Bake cookies for 12–15 minutes or until slightly golden on the bottoms.

Yield: 24 cookies

Nutrition Information (per cookie):

110 calories; 8.3 g. fat; 8 mg. cholesterol; 57 mg. sodium; 7.6 g. carbohydrate; 3.3 g. fiber; 2.9 g. protein; 4.7 g. sugar

Cook's Comment:

Be sure to use a high-quality, blanched almond flour for this recipe in particular. The cookies can become grainy if a poor-quality almond flour is used.

Strawberry Rhubarb Pie with Coconut-Almond Crumble

Crust:

2 cups blanched almond flour

¼ teaspoon salt

1 egg

2 tablespoons cold butter, cut into small cubes

Olive oil cooking spray

Filling:

1 lb fresh strawberries, diced

12 oz. fresh rhubarb, diced

⅔ cup sucanat or other granular sugar

½ cup tapioca starch

1 teaspoon pure vanilla extract

1 teaspoon freshly squeezed lemon juice

Crumble:

½ cup blanched almond flour

¼ teaspoon cinnamon

1 tablespoon coconut oil, melted

1 tablespoon honey

Not all rhubarb recipes have to be laden with sugar. Use less sugar paired with summer's sweetest strawberries to bring out fruit's natural sweetness. This pie has a perfect balance of tart and sweet and is best served chilled.

Directions:

Preheat oven to 350° F.

To prepare the crust, pulse the almond flour and salt together in a food processor several times. Add the egg and cold butter and continue to process until the mixture looks moist and pebbly. Spray a pie pan with olive oil cooking spray and transfer the crust to the pan. Using your hands, press the dough into the pan and work the dough up the sides of the pie pan about 1 inch. Using the prongs of a fork, lightly poke the bottom of the pie crust in several places. Par-bake the crust for 10 minutes; remove from the oven and allow to cool.

Meanwhile, combine all of the ingredients for the filling in a large bowl. Allow mixture to rest for 5–10 minutes as natural juices collect in the bottom of the bowl. Using a slotted spoon, transfer the fruit filling to the par-baked and cooled crust and bake for 20 minutes.

While pie is baking, mix the crumble ingredients in a small bowl using a fork. After 20 minutes of baking, sprinkle the crumble mixture over the pie and bake an additional 10–15 minutes.

Remove pie from oven and allow to cool completely before serving. Store pie in refrigerator if not serving immediately.

Yield: 8 slices

Nutrition Information (per slice):

375 calories; 22.6 g. fat; 31 mg. cholesterol; 94 mg. sodium; 40.8 g. carbohydrate; 5.8 g. fiber; 8.8 g. protein; 22.9 g. sugar

Nutrition Note:

Lemon Bars

Crust:
3 cups blanched almond flour
½ teaspoon salt
4½ tablespoons unsalted butter,
     cubed
6 tablespoons honey

Lemon topping:
3 eggs
¾ cup granulated sugar
½ cup freshly squeezed lemon
     juice (about 3 lemons)
3 tablespoons tapioca starch

Cook's Comment:

Be sure to press the dough evenly into the bottom of the pan, otherwise the lemon filling will not be evenly distributed over the entire crust surface. Use the back of a spatula to best achieve that even layer.

Directions:

Preheat oven to 350° F. Mist an 8 x 8-inch baking dish with cooking spray and set aside.

In the bowl of a food processor, pulse together the almond flour and salt. Drop the cubed butter into the processor, one at a time, pulsing between each addition. Stream the honey into the food processor, pulsing in quick intervals and processing until mixture resembles rough gravel. Transfer the mixture to the baking dish, and using the back of a spatula, firmly press the crust into an even layer, reaching the sides and corners of the dish. Bake for 15–17 minutes or until just beginning to turn golden; remove from oven.

Reduce oven temperature to 325° F.

Whisk the eggs and sugar together in a medium bowl; beat well. Add the lemon juice and mix well. Whisk in the tapioca starch and mix well to remove any lumps. Pour the lemon mixture over the crust and bake for 20 minutes. Remove and allow to cool to room temperature, then transfer to the refrigerator for at least 2 hours. Cut and serve chilled.

Yield: 16 lemon bars

Nutrition Information (per bar):

226 calories; 14.6 g. fat; 43 mg. cholesterol; 93 mg. sodium; 21.9 g. carbohydrate; 2.3 g. fiber; 5.6 g. protein; 16.4 g. sugar

Baklava Custard Ice Cream

1 cup heavy whipping cream
1 cup whole milk
¾ cup sugar, divided
3 large egg yolks
1 cup nonfat plain Greek yogurt

Pinch of salt
1 teaspoon coconut oil
½ cup almond flour
½ cup pistachios
¼ cup honey

Directions:

Combine heavy whipping cream, whole milk, and ½ cup sugar in heavy medium saucepan. Bring mixture to a simmer, stirring until sugar dissolves.

Whisk 3 large egg yolks and remaining ¼ cup sugar in large, heatproof bowl until blended. Gradually add hot cream mixture to yolk mixture and whisk until blended.

Return mixture to saucepan and stir over medium-low heat until custard thickens slightly and coats the back of a spoon, about 3 minutes. Do not allow mixture to boil. Transfer custard back to the heatproof bowl.

Place bowl with custard in larger bowl filled halfway with ice and water. Whisk occasionally until custard is almost cool to touch, about 10 minutes. Once cooled, whisk the yogurt and pinch of salt into custard. Refrigerate custard until well chilled, at least several hours.

Meanwhile, heat the oil in a small skillet over medium heat. Once melted, add the almond flour and toast for 1–2 minutes. Add the pistachios and toast an additional 2–3 minutes or until the almond flour begins to brown. Transfer the flour and nuts to a small bowl and stir in honey; set aside to thicken.

Transfer custard to ice cream maker and process according to manufacturer's instructions, adding the almond flour mixture in the last few minutes of churning. Transfer yogurt ice cream to freezer container. Cover and freeze until ice cream is firm. Keep frozen.

Yield: 4 cups (8 servings; ½ cup each)

Nutrition Information (per ½ cup):

343 calories; 20.3 g. fat; 123 mg. cholesterol; 71 mg. sodium; 35.1 g. carbohydrate; 1.5 g. fiber; 8.0 g. protein; 30.1 g. sugar

Fun Fact:

There is one sinful recipe in this book . . . this is it! I was experimenting with almond flour and came up with this idea. The recipe was too perfect to alter, and I quickly shared the ice cream with friends who demanded the recipe. Enjoy . . . on occasion.

Dark Chocolate and Almond Rice Krispie Treats

Cooking spray

3 tablespoons unsalted butter

10 oz. gluten-free, vegetarian mini marshmallows

6 cups gluten-free rice krispies cereal

12 oz. dark chocolate morsels

2 tablespoons coconut oil

½ cup blanched almond flour

3 tablespoons almond slivers

Directions:

Spray a 9 x 13-inch baking dish with cooking spray and set aside.

In a large pot, melt the butter over medium-high heat. Once melted, lower the heat slightly and stir in marshmallows. Every 1–2 minutes, stir marshmallows with a heat-safe rubber spatula.

Once marshmallows are melted into the butter, fold in the rice krispies. Transfer the mixture to the baking dish and, using the back side of a large spatula wet with cold water to prevent sticking, press the mixture down into the baking dish. Press the mixture into an even layer, reaching the sides and corners of the baking dish.

In a microwave-safe bowl, combine the chocolate morsels and coconut oil. Microwave on high 2–4 minutes, stirring every 30 seconds until melted and smooth; stir in the almond flour. Spread the chocolate mixture over the rice krispies and spread evenly over the entire surface using an offset knife. Sprinkle the almond slivers over the top and allow chocolate to set, about 30–45 minutes.

Cut into squares and serve.

Yield: 28 2 x 2-inch squares

Nutrition Information (per square):

151 calories; 7.6 g. fat; 3 mg. cholesterol; 60 mg. sodium; 21.6 g. carbohydrate; 1.2 g. fiber; 1.7 g. protein; 12.5 g. sugar

Cook's Comment:

A rice krispie treat can only be improved with a layer of chocolate covering its top side. Add coconut oil for a glossy, firm finish and almond flour for fiber, heart-healthy fat, and a unique texture.

Shopping Tip:

Any marshmallow will work in this recipe, but to keep this dessert truly vegan, look for vegan marshmallows.

Pineapple Upside-Down Cake

¹/₃ cup + ¼ cup brown sugar, divided

5 fresh pineapple slices, ¼-inch thick

2½ cups blanched almond flour

2 teaspoons baking powder

½ teaspoon salt

4 tablespoons unsalted butter, softened

3 eggs

1 teaspoon vanilla

8 oz. crushed pineapple, drained

Cook's Comment:

This cake is incredibly moist. Be sure to store leftovers in the fridge for up to three days. It is best served soon after baking.

Directions:

Preheat oven to 350° F.

Mist a 10-inch spring-form pan with nonstick cooking spray. Sprinkle ¼ cup brown sugar on the bottom of the pan and arrange the pineapple slices over the sugar (they will overlap). Set pan aside.

In a medium bowl, whisk together the almond flour, baking powder, and salt; set aside.

In a large bowl using an electric hand mixer or in the bowl of a stand mixer, cream together the butter and remaining 1/3 cup brown sugar on medium speed until light and fluffy, about 2 minutes. Add the eggs, one at a time, mixing 30–60 seconds after each egg to incorporate well. Add the vanilla and mix an additional 20–30 seconds.

Slowly incorporate the almond flour into the wet ingredients, mixing well. Fold in the crushed pineapple.

Carefully transfer the batter to the spring-form pan on top of the pineapple slices. Spread the batter to the edges of the pan and smooth the top using the back of a spoon or spatula.

Bake cake for 40 minutes or until golden. Remove from oven and allow cake to cool completely on a wire cooling rack. Run a knife around the edge of the pan before releasing the spring and removing the ring from the base. Place a plate, upside down, on top of the cake and carefully flip the cake to have the pineapple rings on top; carefully remove the base.

Yield: 10 slices

Nutrition Information (per slice):

284 calories; 19.9 g. fat; 68 mg. cholesterol; 242 mg. sodium; 22.6 g. carbohydrate; 3.4 g. fiber; 8.1 g. protein; 16.6 g. sugar

Chocolate S'mores Cookies

1½ cups blanched almond flour

¼ cup coconut flour

¼ cup unsweetened cocoa powder

¼ teaspoon salt

¼ teaspoon baking soda

¼ cup unsalted butter, at room temperature

¼ cup granulated sugar

2 eggs

1 teaspoon vanilla extract

⅓ cup chocolate chips

½ cup vegan mini marshmallows

½ cup gluten-free rice krispie cereal

Directions:

Preheat oven to 350° F.

In a medium bowl, whisk together the almond flour, coconut flour, cocoa powder, salt, and baking soda.

In the bowl of a stand mixer fitted with the paddle attachment or in a large bowl using an electric hand mixer on medium speed, cream together the room temperature butter and sugar for 2–3 minutes or until light and fluffy. Add the eggs, one at a time, mixing between additions. Add the vanilla and beat an additional 30–60 seconds.

Slowly add the dry ingredients into the butter mixture, mixing after each addition until mixture is consistent throughout. Fold in the chocolate chips, marshmallows, and cereal.

Roll tablespoon-sized balls of dough and place onto cookie sheets, leaving 1–2 inches between cookies. Using the palm of your hand, slightly flatten the dough.

Bake cookies for 11–12 minutes. Allow to cool completely before removing from the cookie sheets.

Yield: 24 cookies

Nutrition Information (per cookie):

99 calories; 6.8 g. fat; 20 mg. cholesterol; 51 mg. sodium; 8.0 g. carbohydrate; 1.6 g. fiber; 2.5 g. protein; 3.0 g. sugar

Cook's Comment:

Bake the cookies immediately after mixing the dough. The rice krispies offer up a unique texture after baking.

Blueberry-Peach Galette

Crust:

2 cups blanched almond flour

½ cup buckwheat flour

½ cup tapioca flour

½ teaspoon baking soda

½ teaspoon salt

¼ cup sucanat or granulated sugar

4 tablespoons cold butter, cubed

2 eggs

Filling:

2 peaches, sliced

1 tablespoon tapioca flour

2 cups blueberries

2 tablespoons sucanat

Cook's Comment:

Despite its name, buckwheat is gluten-free and does not contain wheat. It is often touted as one of the easiest gluten-free flours to use, and its unique gray-blue hue gives baked goods a fun coloration.

Directions:

Combine almond flour, buckwheat flour, tapioca flour, baking soda, salt, and sucanat in the bowl of a food processor and pulse 10–20 times to combine. Add the cubed butter and eggs, pulsing to combine. The crust will be slightly putty-like in consistency. Turn dough onto a piece of parchment paper and form into a ball. Wrap the dough in plastic wrap and refrigerate for 1–2 hours, or longer.

Meanwhile, combine the sliced peaches and tapioca flour in a medium bowl; toss well to distribute. Add the blueberries and sucanat, and toss well.

Preheat oven to 375° F.

Once refrigerated, roll the crust into a 20- to 24-inch round, about ¼-inch thick, on a piece of parchment paper. The edges may be delicate, but can be pieced back together. Transfer the parchment paper with the dough onto a baking sheet or pizza pan. Pile the fruit into the middle of the crust, spreading to about 2–3 inches from the corners. Fold the crust edges up and over the fruit.

Bake galette for 35–40 minutes or until bubbly and slightly browned. Serve warm or at room temperature.

Yield: 10 pieces

Nutrition Information (per ¹⁄₁₀):

280 calories; 16.9 g. fat; 49.0 mg. cholesterol; 197 mg. sodium; 28.9 g. carbohydrate; 4.7 g. fiber; 7.3 g. protein; 5.2 g. sugar

Strawberry Balsamic Shortcakes

Shortcakes:
2½ cups blanched almond flour
2 teaspoons baking powder
½ teaspoon salt
¼ cup (½ stick) unsalted butter
1 tablespoon honey
2 large eggs

Balsamic Strawberries:
1½ lbs strawberries, hulled and
    roughly chopped
3 tablespoons white balsamic
    vinegar
2 tablespoons honey
1 tablespoon potato starch
2 cups whipped cream

Cook's Comment:

Potato starch is a strong thickening agent. Avoid over-cooking the strawberries as to not have a gummy consistency to the liquid.

Directions:

Preheat oven to 350° F. Line a baking sheet with parchment paper and set aside.

For the shortcakes, combine the almond flour, baking powder, and salt in a large bowl; whisk well.

In a separate microwave-safe bowl, melt the butter in the microwave on high for 20–40 seconds, checking every 5–10 seconds. Once butter is melted, whisk in the honey. Allow mixture to cool a few moments, then whisk in the eggs. Add the egg mixture to the dry ingredients and stir to combine thoroughly.

Drop the biscuits by rounded ⅛ cups onto the lined baking sheet and flatten slightly, using your fingers.

Bake the shortcakes 12–15 minutes or until slightly golden.

Meanwhile, combine the strawberries, vinegar, and honey in a small sauce pan over medium-high heat. Stirring often, heat the ingredients for 5–6 minutes or until strawberries have softened. Add the potato starch to the pan and stir well, allowing juices to thicken for about 1 minute. Remove from heat.

Cut the shortcakes in half; top each bottom half with 3–4 tablespoons of strawberry mixture and then 2 generous tablespoons of whipped cream. Add the top half of the shortcake and serve immediately.

Yield: 10 strawberry shortcakes

Nutrition Information (per shortcake, as prepared):

285 calories; 21.8 g. fat; 57 mg. cholesterol; 235 mg. sodium; 20.3 g. carbohydrate; 5.0 g. fiber; 7.7 g. protein; 12.4 g. sugar

Pecan, Pumpkin, and Chocolate Mini Pies

Crusts:

2 cups blanched almond flour

¼ teaspoon salt

1 tablespoon granulated sugar

1 egg

2 tablespoons unsalted butter, cubed

Filling:

2 tablespoons unsalted butter

¹/₃ cup brown sugar

¼ cup pure maple syrup

¼ teaspoon salt

²/₃ cup pecans, chopped

2 eggs

1 teaspoon vanilla extract

¹/₃ cup pumpkin purée

2 tablespoons mini chocolate chips

Nutrition Note:

Pecan pie is my favorite. Unfortunately, it doesn't offer much in the way of nutrition. By using almond flour, pumpkin, and far less butter and sugar, this recipe is not only gluten-free and high in fiber, but it also tastes great and offers a nutritional edge over a traditional pecan pie.

Directions:

Preheat oven to 350° F. Mist six mini (4-inch) pie pans with nonstick cooking spray; set aside.

To prepare the crust, pulse the almond flour, salt, and sugar together in a food processor several times. Add the egg and cold butter and continue to pulse to process the mixture until it becomes moist and pebbly.

Distribute the dough between the six pie pans, and using your fingers, work the dough evenly along the bottom of the tins and up the sides, flush with the tops of the tins. Arrange muffin tins on a baking sheet and bake crusts 8 minutes; remove and allow to cool.

Meanwhile, combine the butter, brown sugar, syrup, and salt in a small sauce pan over medium heat. Bring to a boil and reduce heat to simmer and thicken slightly, about 5–6 minutes. Stir in pecans and remove from heat; allow to cool for about 10 minutes.

In a small bowl, whisk together the vanilla, eggs, and pumpkin purée. Once syrup mixture has cooled, slowly incorporate it into the egg mixture, whisking constantly. Mix well.

Distribute 1 teaspoon of mini chocolate chips to the bottom of each pie and top with the filling, distributing the filling evenly among the six pies.

Bake pies for 25 minutes and allow to cool before removing from the tins to serve.

Yield: 6 mini pies (12 servings; ½ pie each)

Nutrition Information (per serving):

254 calories; 19.3 g. fat; 56 mg. cholesterol; 122 mg. sodium; 17.5 g. carbohydrate; 6.3 g. fiber; 6.2 g. protein; 10.8 g. sugar

Key Lime Pie Bites

Crust:
2 cups blanched almond flour

¼ teaspoon salt

1 egg

2 tablespoons cold butter, cut into small cubes

Olive oil cooking spray

Filling:
½ cup key lime juice from ~¾ lb key limes (about 30 limes)

½ cup 2% plain Greek yogurt

14 oz. can low-fat sweetened condensed milk

3 egg yolks

2 drops green food dye (optional)

Cook's Comment:

If you cannot find key limes, use limes. Key limes are sweeter than limes, but they can be used interchangeably in this recipe.

Directions:

Preheat oven to 350° F. Mist two mini muffin tins with nonstick cooking spray; set aside.

To prepare the crust, pulse the almond flour and salt together in a food processor several times. Add the egg and cold butter and continue to process until the mixture looks moist and pebbly.

Using 1 heaping teaspoon of dough in each mini muffin well, use your fingers to work the dough up the sides of the well in an even, thin layer. Repeat with remaining wells, filling 40 wells with dough. Bake the crusts for 8–9 minutes and remove from oven; allow to cool completely.

In the bowl of a stand mixer or a large bowl with a hand mixer, beat all of the filling ingredients together on medium speed for 2 minutes.

Once the crusts are cooled, carefully spoon scant tablespoonfuls of the key lime pie filling into each crust. Bake the pie bites for 12–15 minutes. Allow to cool to room temperature, then transfer to the fridge to set for 1–2 hours before serving.

Yield: 40 mini key lime pie bites

Nutrition Information (per bite):

76 calories; 4.3 g. fat; 22 mg. cholesterol; 34 mg. sodium; 7.9 g. carbohydrate; 0.6 g. fiber; 2.9 g. protein; 6.6 g. sugar

Almond Butter Swirl Brownies

5 oz. 80% cacao chocolate,
   broken into pieces
½ cup coconut oil
½ cup honey

5 eggs
¼ teaspoon salt
¾ cup blanched almond flour
¹/₃ cup natural almond butter

Directions:

Preheat oven to 375° F.

In a small sauce pan over medium-low heat, melt the chocolate and coconut oil, whisking often. Once melted and combined, remove from heat and whisk in the honey; allow to cool for 10–15 minutes.

One by one, whisk in the eggs. Add the salt and almond flour; mix well.

Pour the batter into an 8 x 8-inch baking dish that has been coated with nonstick cooking spray. Drop the almond butter by spoonfuls onto the surface of the brownie batter. Using a knife, swirl the almond butter through the brownie batter.

Bake for 20–22 minutes or until set. Allow to cool before slicing. Store leftovers in the refrigerator.

Yield: 16 brownies

Nutrition Information (per brownie):

223 calories; 18.3 g. fat; 58 mg. cholesterol; 86 mg. sodium; 12.8 g. carbohydrate; 2.3 g. fiber; 5.2 g. protein; 10.6 g. sugar

Fun Fact:

Peanuts are a legume and thus are not Paleo. Alternately, almond butter is used in this recipe to create a Paleo brownie delight!

Ooey Gooey Chocolate Chip and Flax Cookies

1¼ cups blanched almond flour
¼ cup ground flaxseed
½ teaspoon baking powder
¼ teaspoon salt
¼ cup brown sugar, packed
1 egg
¼ cup coconut oil, melted and slightly cooled
1 teaspoon pure vanilla extract
¼ cup mini 70% cocoa dark chocolate chips

Directions:

In a large bowl, whisk to combine the almond flour, flaxseed, baking powder, salt, and brown sugar.

In a separate bowl, lightly beat the egg. Add the melted coconut oil slowly to the egg, whisking constantly; whisk in the vanilla.

Fold the wet ingredients into the dry; fold in the chocolate chips. Cover bowl with plastic wrap and refrigerate for at least 30 minutes.

Preheat oven to 375° F. Line two baking sheets with parchment paper and set aside.

Once chilled, roll the dough into 1-inch balls and arrange on baking sheets. Slightly flatten cookies to about ¾-inch thickness.

Bake cookies 7–9 minutes or until dry-looking and slightly browned. Allow to cool 2–3 minutes on the baking sheet before transferring to a cooling rack to cool completely.

Yield: 16 cookies

Nutrition Information (per cookie):

125 calories; 9.9 g. fat; 12 mg. cholesterol; 58 mg. sodium; 7.9 g. carbohydrate; 1.5 g. fiber; 2.8 g. protein; 3.3 g. sugar

Cook's Comment:

These cookies do not leaven much, so there's no need to space them out more than an inch apart on the baking sheet. Great things can come in small packages!

Cinnamon Apple Tart

Crust:

2 cups blanched almond flour

¼ teaspoon salt

2 tablespoons granulated sugar

½ teaspoon cinnamon

1 egg

2 tablespoons unsalted butter, cubed

Filling:

5 apples, peeled, cored, and thinly sliced

3 egg yolks

¾ cup nonfat plain Greek yogurt

¾ cup granulated sugar

2 tablespoons tapioca flour

1 teaspoon cinnamon

Cook's Comment:

The tangy yogurt in this recipe replaces sour cream in a traditional tart. By using a nonfat Greek yogurt variety, you not only reduce the calories, but you also increase the amount of protein in the recipe.

Directions:

Preheat oven to 350° F.

Mist a 10-inch tart pan with cooking spray and place a 10-inch round piece of parchment paper in the bottom of the pan. Mist top of paper with cooking spray and set aside.

To prepare the crust, pulse the almond flour, salt, sugar, and cinnamon together in a food processor several times. Add the egg and cold butter and continue to pulse to process the mixture until it looks moist and pebbly.

Transfer the dough to the tart pan and, using your fingers, work the dough evenly along the bottom of the tin and up the side until it is flush with the top of the tin. Poke 6–7 series of holes in the bottom of the crust using a fork and bake crust for 8–10 minutes or until it looks slightly dried out.

Arrange the apple slices in the bottom of the par-baked crust. Note: the apple slices will be heaping, but will cook down.

In a medium bowl, whisk together the yolks, yogurt, sugar, tapioca flour, and cinnamon until well combined. Slowly pour the filling over the apples, allowing it to seep into the nooks and crannies of the apples.

Bake tart for 55–65 minutes or until golden brown. Allow to cool completely on a wire rack before slicing and serving.

Yield: 10 slices

Nutrition Information (per slice):

288 calories; 15.6 g. fat; 88 mg. cholesterol; 82 mg. sodium; 32.1 g. carbohydrate; 3.6 g. fiber; 8.0 g. protein; 25.3 g. sugar

Index

Conversion Charts

Metric and Imperial Conversions

(These conversions are rounded for convenience)

Ingredient	Cups/Tablespoons/Teaspoons	Ounces	Grams/Milliliters
Butter	1 cup/ 16 tablespoons/ 2 sticks	8 ounces	230 grams
Cheese, shredded	1 cup	4 ounces	110 grams
Cream cheese	1 tablespoon	0.5 ounce	14.5 grams
Cornstarch	1 tablespoon	0.3 ounce	8 grams
Flour, all-purpose	1 cup/1 tablespoon	4.5 ounces/0.3 ounce	125 grams/8 grams
Flour, whole wheat	1 cup	4 ounces	120 grams
Fruit, dried	1 cup	4 ounces	120 grams
Fruits or veggies, chopped	1 cup	5 to 7 ounces	145 to 200 grams
Fruits or veggies, pureed	1 cup	8.5 ounces	245 grams
Honey, maple syrup, or corn syrup	1 tablespoon	0.75 ounce	20 grams
Liquids: cream, milk, water, or juice	1 cup	8 fluid ounces	240 milliliters
Oats	1 cup	5.5 ounces	150 grams
Salt	1 teaspoon	0.2 ounce	6 grams
Spices: cinnamon, cloves, ginger, or nutmeg (ground)	1 teaspoon	0.2 ounce	5 milliliters
Sugar, brown, firmly packed	1 cup	7 ounces	200 grams
Sugar, white	1 cup/1 tablespoon	7 ounces/0.5 ounce	200 grams/12.5 grams
Vanilla extract	1 teaspoon	0.2 ounce	4 grams

Oven Temperatures

Fahrenheit	Celsius	Gas Mark
225°	110°	$1/4$
250°	120°	$1/2$
275°	140°	1
300°	150°	2
325°	160°	3
350°	180°	4
375°	190°	5
400°	200°	6
425°	220°	7
450°	230°	8